FIELD AND INFORMATION GUIDE TO RAPTOR'S VIEW AND THE KRUGER TO CANYONS BIOSPHERE REGION

Southern Cross Schools

The Baobab
(*Adansonia digitata*)
is one of the largest and best
known trees of the world. It is
found northwards from about the
Tropic of Capricorn, throughout
the Lowveld.

ACKNOWLEDGEMENTS

Most Jacana Maps and Guides are the result of team work, and our Lowveld publication is no exception. Major thanks to the High Branching team of Nicky Caverhill, Paule Sachs, Denise Raikin, Peter and Val Thomas and Deborah White. The inhouse Jacana team were invaluable, and our thanks specifically to Janet Bartlet, Mike Martin, Bambi Nunes, Jennifer Prangley, Rangee Ramsamy and Brett Rogers. For scientific editing and input, thank you to Duan Biggs, Jane Carruthers, Rina Grant, John Rushworth, Charles Stuart and Clive Webber. Thanks are due, for editing, to Lesley Emmanuel and John Deane; for DTP and design consultancy thanks to Heather Kruger, Georgina MacRobert, Laurel McBirnie, and Anina Kruger. Mapping was done by Lourens du Plessis at Metrogis. New art in this publication was done by Penny Noall and Joan van Gogh, and all photographs are individually acknowledged.

Dung Beetle
(Family Scarabaeidae)
page 21

Published by: ©Jacana Media (Pty) Ltd, Johannesburg, 2004
PO Box 2004, Houghton 2041, Johannesburg, South Africa
Tel: (011) 648-1157; Fax: (011) 648-5516
E-mail: marketing@jacana.co.za; Website: www.jacana.co.za
Created and developed by High Branching (Pty) Ltd
Tel: (011) 728-6937; Fax: (011) 483-1294
E-mail: val@highbranching.co.za; Website: www.highbranching.co.za
Printing: Fishwicks the Printers, Durban
Cover: Disturbance, Durban

ISBN 1-919931-20-1

Contents

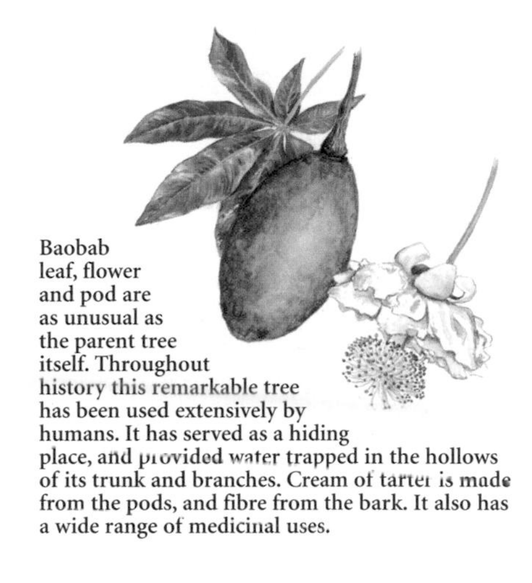

Baobab leaf, flower and pod are as unusual as the parent tree itself. Throughout history this remarkable tree has been used extensively by humans. It has served as a hiding place, and provided water trapped in the hollows of its trunk and branches. Cream of tarter is made from the pods, and fibre from the bark. It also has a wide range of medicinal uses.

PETER THOMAS

Impala cautiously move downslope, towards water in the early morning sunlight.

LOWVELD

The term Lowveld has two different connotations:

- The first concept relates to the climate, landform and geology. It refers to the area that is below 1 000 m, stretching from northern KwaZulu-Natal well into Zimbabwe.
- The second concept refers to a popular tourist area. In the south this encompasses Komatipoort, Nelspruit and Barberton. On the west it is bounded by the foothills of the Drakensberg, all the way north to the Limpopo River. This concept of 'Lowveld' includes all of the Kruger National Park, even though areas of the Malelane Mountains and the sandstone ridges round Punda Maria and Pafuri are higher than 1 000 m.

Our definition of the Lowveld includes both of the concepts above. In addition, the Grids of Activity at the back, with the Maps, also cover areas that are above 1 000 m. These Grids help the visitor to discover the magic of the entire area.

This book is designed to enable you to plan your route according to your interests. It allows identification of animals and plants that are easy to find and/or are spectacular. It includes interpretation of how they interact with one another and their environment.

The major rivers of the Lowveld flow from west to east, and are the lifeblood for many animals and plants.

VAL THOMAS

Creation of Landscapes

Apart from the impact of humans, the landscape is formed by interaction of the following:

- ***Geology** – through weathering and erosion, forming soils that provide nutrients*
- ***Climate** – temperature, wind and rainfall*
- ***Animals** – from small termites to large plant-eaters such as elephant*
- ***Fire** – naturally occurring and man-made*

The type of soil and amount of rainfall determines how much food and water will be available, and thus the variety of animals and plants that will occur in the area. The amount of grass, and the height and density of the trees and shrubs are affected by both animals and fire.

Water gradually erodes rocks, and carves out gorges along the major rivers.

Geology – Weathering, Erosion and Soils

The fundamental process of rock converting to soil is the same worldwide, irrespective of the geology that forms the base. Over millions of years, parent rock is very, very slowly eroded by seeping rainwater and wind, and by heat and cold.

These actions break off pieces that range between huge boulders and minute particles, from the original rock. The smaller segments are carried away by water, and gradually broken down further into grains of sand which are chemically similar to the parent rock.

The process of erosion and weathering, and the resultant shape of the land, varies greatly, depending on the initial rock type. The main types of rock, and consequent landform and soils of the Lowveld, are granite, gabbro, Ecca Shales, basalt, rhyolite and sandstone.

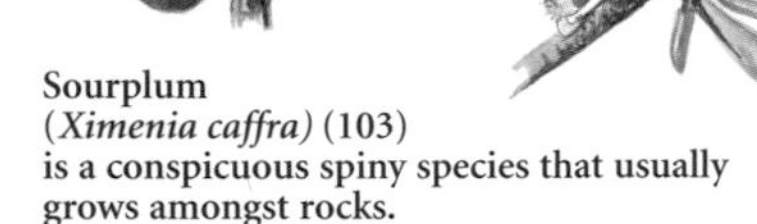

Sourplum (*Ximenia caffra*) (103) is a conspicuous spiny species that usually grows amongst rocks.

Climate

The Lowveld is a semi-arid zone with summer rainfall of 200-600 mm per year. This decreases from west to east and from south to north. The summers are hot and humid with temperatures of up to 44°C. Winters are mild and dry.

The rivers are fed from 4 main catchment areas of the Drakensberg and the Highveld. The waters carried by them are life-giving arteries essential for the survival of many animals. In the Lowveld, major floods occur sporadically in variable cycles of about 30 years, and can alter the landscapes along the major rivers, as well as along some of the smaller drainage lines.

Common Platanna (*Xenopus laevis*) is totally aquatic, venturing onto dry land only when moving to another body of water.

Floods sometimes create a new landscape, uprooting trees that can be hundreds of years old.

Animals

Every animal in Africa plays its part in the greater scheme of interaction and survival in their environment.

Millions of little creatures pollinate plants to ensure the vegetation is able to reproduce and play its role. There are termites that are the prime maintainers of the quality of the soil underground. There are also the vast numbers of herbivores that eat and digest the plants and return fertiliser to the earth. The very large plant-eaters – elephant, buffalo, rhino and hippo – process such staggering amounts of plant material during their lives that the entire balance of woody material, grass and soft vegetation is affected, if they are not around.

Sunspiders (page 32) are not true spiders, as they lack both silk and poison glands. They are completely harmless to humans.

The sheer numbers of antelope can change any landscape – a stark reality when a relatively rainless period reduces the vegetation available for food. Dry, dusty stretches of brown, sandy earth appear within weeks if there has been insufficient rainfall. It soon becomes apparent that drought is to be feared, not only because of the lack of water to drink, but more importantly, because food runs out, and the animals remove the plant life that binds the soil.

PETER THOMAS

Buffalo herds alter landscapes as they eat their way through grasslands, and churn up pans and river banks while drinking.

Fire

Natural fires have altered the landscapes of Africa for millions of years. They are mainly caused by lightning strikes. Since time immemorial, natural fires have reduced the spread of certain plants and animals, and encouraged the growth and survival of others.

Guineafowl Butterflies (*Hamanumida daedalus*) (60 mm) are visible all year round.

As dry grass and woody vegetation build up a significant load of dead organic matter, the chance of fire increases until it becomes virtually inevitable.

Once humans discovered the uses of fire, and added both their accidents and their intentions to the formula, regular burns became an even more certain fact of life in the wild.

Scientists throughout the continent are working on a vast variety of ways of ensuring diversity and the maintenence of a sustainable future for all species, despite fences, interference and pollution. They are trying to establish the best ways to handle fires to maintain the natural eco-system and its processes. (There is more information on fire on page xx.)

VAL THOMAS

Fires are a natural part of the cycle of life in the Lowveld, but many animals like this steenbok, suffer when a hot fire rages through.

Lowveld Landform

The simplest way of visualising the Lowveld landform is to divide it into four longitudinal sections. These are shown on the map on the opposite page.

1. *Down the western boundary, various hills and mountains are higher than the rest of the Lowveld area. This section includes the northen sandstone hills of Punda Maria, the central Drakensberg foothills, and in the south both the Malelane and Barberton mountains.*
2. *Still on the west are old, tough granites which have eroded to an undulating terrain of rolling hills.*
3. *On the east are younger, softer Ecca Shales, gabbro and basalt. All three erode to form flat, clay plains.*
4. *The eastern boundary is rhyolite-based, forming the Lebombo Mountains.*

The plains of the eastern side of the Lowveld occur inside Kruger, and the wide open spaces offer special opportunities for viewing game.

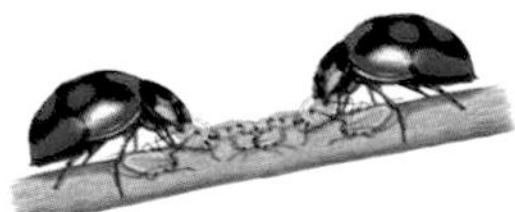

Ladybirds (Family Coccinellidae) are an essential link in the animal/plant chain of the Lowveld.

Ecozones

The four sections described above, and shown on the map, are a simple visual summary to offer you an instant overview. In reality, the Lowveld is a large area of hundreds of kilometres both north to south and east to west. The rainfall, altitude and latitude significantly alter the natural sequences within each major group.

Therefore to understand the animals and plants that thrive here, we have further divided the area into 15 Ecozones. These are shown on the maps on pages 104 - 112. Each Ecozone is represented by different colours, letters and names, and these are used in the discussions on the descriptive pages viii to xxi that follow. As you travel through the Lowveld, there is enough detail to help you understand the natural interactions of plants, animals and even humans. Features that occur throughout the area, such as water, rocky and burnt areas and temite mounds, are also covered.

Narina Trogon (*Apaloderma narina*) are rare, secretive, exquisite birds of riverine and evergreen forests.

The spectacular view from the Olifants Rest Camp in Kruger allows you to see a number of Ecozones – from the flat basalt plains, to the rocks of the rhyolite Lebombos, and even the distant granite hills.

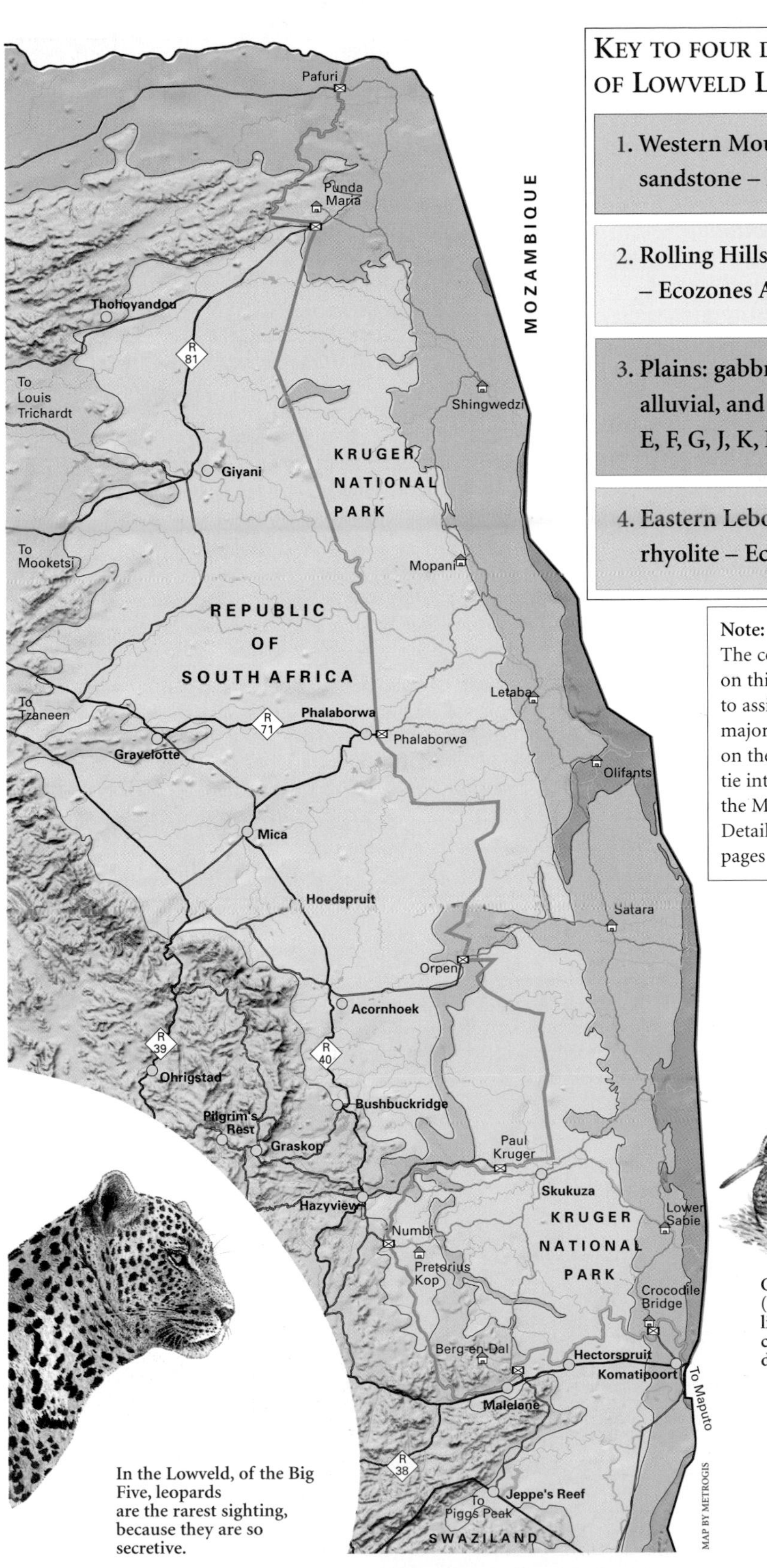

In the Lowveld, of the Big Five, leopards are the rarest sighting, because they are so secretive.

Key to four divisions of Lowveld Landform

1. Western Mountains: granite and sandstone – Ecozones C and N

2. Rolling Hills: granite – Ecozones A, B, D and P

3. Plains: gabbro, basalt, Ecca Shales, alluvial, and sandstone – Ecozones E, F, G, J, K, L, M, N and O

4. Eastern Lebombo Mountains: rhyolite – Ecozones I and J

Note:
The colours used on the map on this page are ONLY provided to assist in identifying the four major Landform divisions discussed on the previous page. They do not tie into the Ecozone colours, nor the Map Grid colours, in any way. Detailed maps are on pages 104 - 111.

Greater Painted-Snipe (*Rostratula benghalensis*) live in wet areas with adequate plant cover, and are easily overlooked despite their beautiful colouring.

Rolling Hills of Granite

Imagine a huge area covered by one vast outcrop of rock. Over millions of years, rainwater causes cracks in this rock, which form gullies and eventually water drainage lines between rolling hills. This is the overall picture of the granite landscapes that can be seen from the air in the western Lowveld.

Rainwater drains easily through the crest soil, carrying debris as well as chemicals and minerals into the valleys. Soils in the low-lying areas are therefore fine-grained, clayey and rich in minerals.

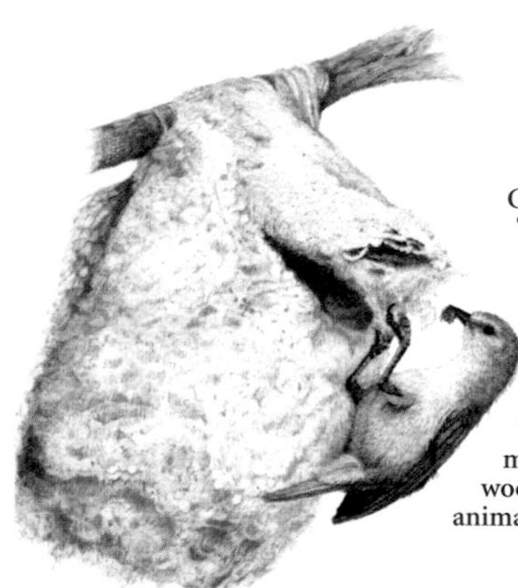

Grey Penduline-Tits (*Anthoscopus caroli*) are relatively tame, and seen in pairs or small groups. Their nests are made of soft, woolly plant and animal matter.

Southern Crests –

Ecozones A, B and D

The soils on the crests of the hills that develop from the ancient granites are coarse, sandy and low in nutrients.

The water seeping downhill from these less fertile crests is like a very thin soup, providing little nourishment for the trees and plant life growing there. The trees therefore take in large volumes of water to obtain sufficient nutrients. Excess water, however, needs to be eliminated. Trees, such as the Bushwillows (*Combretum* species page 5) and Marula (page 3) therefore tend to have larger leaves to increase transpiration, and are referred to as broad-leaved.

Red Grass (*Themeda triandra*) is resistant to fire and enjoyed by grazers.

The large surface area of these leaves is very attractive to insects. Some of the trees protect themselves against insect-foraging by producing chemicals called tannins. These also reduce browsing by mammal herbivores because of their bitter taste, like strong, black tea.

As a result of the coarse-grained, sieve-like, relatively infertile soil, the grasses on the crests tend to be taller and are generally less tasty varieties. These grasses do, however, provide food for bulk grazers, such as buffalo, during the dry season.

The dense groups of trees attract many species of unusual birds including Yellow-bellied Eremomelas and Grey Penduline-Tits. Large trees are ideal nesting places for eagles like Wahlberg's (page 58).

The gently rolling hills add to the excitement, as you never know what is over each crest.

Wild Cotton (*Gossypium herbceum*) is a scrambling shrub that grows in woodland thickets.

Mopane (*Colophospermum mopane*) are the dominant tree throughout the northern granite hills. They are easily recognised as there are literally hundreds of thousands of trees and their leaves are butterfly-shaped.

VAL THOMAS

The undulating hills of Ecozone P stretch as far as the eye can see.

Common River Frog (*Afrana angolensis*) leap into water when disturbed. They live in, and beside streams, and have a croak like a squeaky door.

Northern Crests – Ecozone P

Being granite-based, Ecozone P has undulating hills with many dissecting streams and rivers. This is an important Ecozone for Sable Antelope. They prefer the hilly areas to the flatter basalts, as in the hills there are generally fewer of the antelope, and therefore fewer predators. Large herds of buffalo and breeding herds of elephant are, however, common.

The vegetation is predominantly Mopane (above) on the mid-slopes, with only a few additional tree species. The crests are covered in Red Bushwillow (page 5).

Buffalo (page 19) are either seen in herds or as a few solitary old bulls together. These elderly gentlemen often spend their days near water in the lower valleys.

VAL THOMAS

Valleys in the granites tend to be dominated by large riverine trees, and by Acacia species with thorns, like this young Umbrella Acacia.

Lower Slopes and Valleys – Ecozones A, B, D and P

The nutrient-rich, fine soils in the valleys have a high clay content. The soil tends to have little available water, because the water binds to the clay. The soil is, however, high in nutrients rather like a thick stew. The trees here have fine, small leaves, which limit water loss. These trees and associated grasses are highly palatable and are sought after by most antelope.

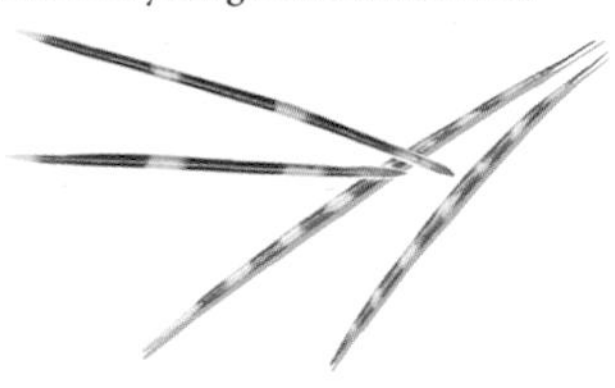

Porcupine quills are beautiful lying in the wild – but not as 'interior design' items.

Open Plains

The base geology, towards the east – between the western granites and the far eastern rhyolites – consists of basalt and Ecca Shales. Here, there are vast, open plains where visitors have a wildlife experience that is completely different from that of the undulating granites. These eastern Lowveld plains of both Mpumalanga and Limpopo Province lie almost entirely within the Kruger National Park. In the southwest, in the Reserves of the greater Kruger Park, are gabbro rockbed areas that also give rise to open plains.

The soils of all these areas are nutrient-rich, finer-grained and high in clay content, compared with the coarse, sandy soils of the granite areas.

Vlei Bristle Grass (*Setaria incrassata*) grows on heavy clays near vleis and marshes.

Animals of the Plains

The plains have fewer trees and shrubs, and greater expanses of 'sweeter' grass. Grazers that thrive here, rely on the unobstructed views to see predators and they often graze in groups of mixed species. This enhances their safety and protection, both through increased numbers and through the variety of sensory awareness. The more eyes, ears and noses that are alert and expert, the more likely are the chances of survival!

Many of the grazers such as zebra, roan and sable, have more distinctive body colouring than their browsing cousins, the kudu and nyala. Patches of light and dark hair accentuate the position of their bodies in territorial displays, while white tails and rump patches are flashed as visual alarm calls, and to facilitate herd-following.

Sticky Acacia (*Acacia borlea*) is aptly named, and is striking because of its shiny leaflets. It is found only in the South African Lowveld.

Secretarybirds (*Sagittarius serpentarius*) stride slowly through the veld, usually in pairs searching for insects, reptiles, rodents and eggs on the ground. They nest on the tops of trees.

VAL THOMAS

A herd of impala grazing on the basalt plains of Ecozone F.

Formation of Pans on Plains

Pans are created when water collects in depressions in the plains, which are high in clay content. There are very few undulations here, and the water has no opportunity to run off. This is very different from the numerous streams and drainage lines of rolling-hill granite.

Pans are maintained, and enlarged, by animal activity such as rhino, buffalo and warthog rolling in the mud. There is more information on pans on page xix.

Red-veined Drop-wing Dragonflies (*Trithemis arteriosa*) are fierce predators – the adults above, and the nymphs below, the water.

SOUTHERN BASALT PLAINS – Ecozones F and K

As noted before, these plains occur almost exclusively within the Kruger National Park. Basalts erode to rich, clay soils, which lead to flat, open, grassy plains. These support many grazers including Blue Wildebeest and zebra.

The rainwater, running into shallow depressions and pans, creates 'wetlands,' ranging from merely damp soil to marsh and water-filled areas. These support a variety of trees, including Fever Tree Acacia (pages 112/113), large Knob Thorn Acacia (page 2) and Marula (page 3). The wetlands are also home to a variety of small creatures like frogs, fish, terrapins and various waterbirds. They also provide water for herds of grazers and the numerous predators that follow them. The open spaces are ideal territory for cheetah, and the abundance of food attracts lion and hyaena.

Lion's Eye (*Tricliceras longipedunculatum*) is a grassland flower with numerous coarse hairs on stems and leaves. The scientific name refers to the pod-shaped, 3-chambered, cylindrical fruit.

In Ecozone K, soils are shallower and the rainfall is lower. Only more drought-resistant trees like Knob Thorn Acacia thrive. Due to a relatively dense grass layer, hot fires occur which prevent the trees from growing taller. In addition, because of the shallow soils and the heavy browsing, the trees generally grow more slowly and are shorter, even in maturity. Many of the Knob Thorns have a conical Christmas-tree appearance. Here you will find one of the highest kudu populations in Kruger as well as numerous giraffe.

The wide open plains of the eastern Ecozones are ideal habitat for grazers.

Guttural Toad (*Bufo gutturalis*) are noisy occupants of the drainage lines and pans. Their call is a vibrant one-second snore, at three-second intervals.

NORTHERN BASALT PLAINS – Ecozone L

The hot, dry, basalt plains north of the Olifants River are dominated by stunted Mopane trees (page ix).

These Mopane are small because their roots are often crimped and broken by the clay expanding and shrinking around them. They can survive most fires, however, by re-sprouting from the base, hence the presence of large, dense stands of equal-sized trees. The wide, grassy drainage lines here are unique, and make this the best area in the Lowveld in which to see rare antelope like roan and tsessebe.

Looking eastward towards the Lebombo Mountains over the basalt plains

Striped Mouse (*Rhabdomys pumilio*) is a grassland species. It burrows near grass clumps, and is active in the early morning and late afternoon. An opportunistic omnivore, it alters its diet seasonally.

Open Plains (Continued)

Interspersed among the dominant rolling-hill landscape of the west, are vast sheets of gabbro.

They are generally the only totally flat expanses of significant size, between the Drakensberg and the edge of the eastern plains. They are the best areas in which to find Square-lipped Rhino and herds of wildebeest and zebra.

Alluvial plains are found along major rivers where they cross the basalts.

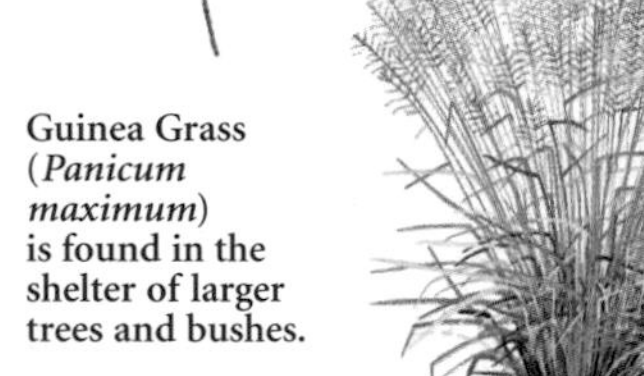

Guinea Grass (*Panicum maximum*) is found in the shelter of larger trees and bushes.

Gabbro - Ecozone E

Gabbro weathers to a clay-like soil that is very rich compared with granite soils. The vegetation is therefore highly nutritious and sought after by both grazers and browsers.

Gabbro plains are superb areas for game watching. Apart from offering less obstructed views, there are opportunities to find larger grassland birds such as Secretarybirds (page x), Kori Bustards and Korhaans (page 43).

Striking block-shaped, dark-grey boulders, some of which rise above the plains in huge outcrops, are a feature of gabbro. Ship Mountain near Pretoriuskop, and Shilawuri further north, are fine examples in Kruger Park. (See page xx for Rocky Areas.)

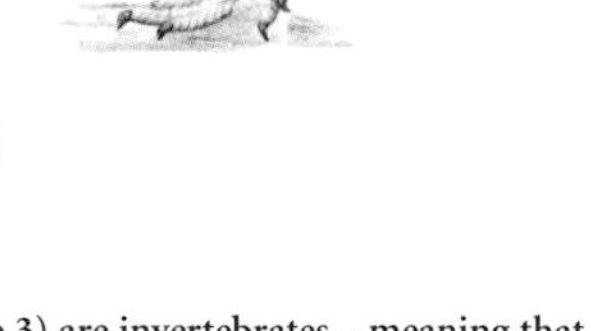

Kori Bustards (*Ardeotis kori*) are residents, but a rare sighting. They walk slowly with marching gait, singly, in pairs or in small groups, and fly reluctantly.

Millipedes (Songololos) (page 3) are invertebrates – meaning that they have no skeleton. They are made of a series of segments which are really two fused body 'rings'. The outer layer is unbendable, and each segment has two pairs of legs. They shed 'skins' occasionally to allow for growth, and are helpless at this time.

Alluvial Plains - Ecozone M

These are floodplains of major rivers, found along the Shingwedzi, Luvuvhu and Limpopo rivers on the eastern side of Kruger.

Before dams became common further upstream, these rivers regularly flooded their banks in high rainfall periods and deposited rich silt along their courses. The flat, sandy-silt terrain and rich soil significantly alters the vegetation and hence the visual experience for visitors.

This is an outstanding game viewing area. Because of the plentiful water and huge trees, both Birders and Tree Spotters will find themselves in a paradise of new species. The massed stands of Narrow-leaved Mustard Trees (*Salvadora australis*) and Fever Tree Acacia forests (pages 112/113) as well as Feverberry Crotons (*Croton megalobotrys*) lining the rivers, are all unique to the area. Forest and riverine birds include African Green-Pigeon (page 50) and Narina Trogon (page vi).

RINA GRANT

The plains around Shingwedzi are visually unique in the Lowveld, and worth visiting for the scenery, as well as for the wildlife there.

The flat, open areas of the Alluvial Plains are ideal cheetah hunting territory.

Southern Ecca Shale Plains – Ecozone G

These plains occur only within the Kruger Park as they are sandwiched between the western rolling hills of granite, and the eastern Lebombo Mountains. They are very different visually, even to the untrained eye, offering relatively flat, open vistas that are not a feature of the granite areas.

The Ecca Shales weather to soft, nutrient-rich soils that sustain highly nutritious plants. As a result, this thin strip carries the highest bio-mass of animal life in Kruger. Visiting the Ecca Shale is a must for all Mammal and Bird Watchers – as well as Tree Spotters. Trees here include the unusual Delagoa Acacia (see below) and Many-stemmed Albizia (*Albizia petersiana*).

VAL THOMAS

Ecozone G carries the greatest bio-mass of animal life in Kruger because of the very palatable vegetation.

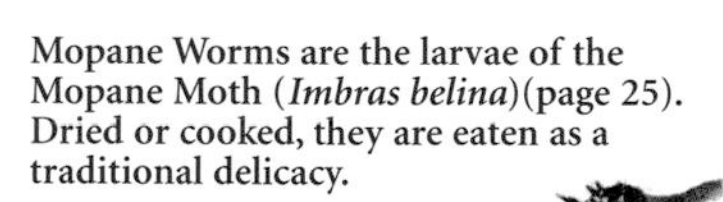

Mopane Worms are the larvae of the Mopane Moth (*Imbras belina*)(page 25). Dried or cooked, they are eaten as a traditional delicacy.

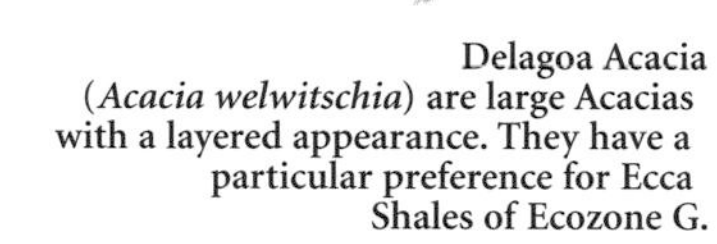

Delagoa Acacia (*Acacia welwitschia*) are large Acacias with a layered appearance. They have a particular preference for Ecca Shales of Ecozone G.

PETER THOMAS

Tall Mopane in the forests in Ecozone O

Northern Ecca Shale Plains – Ecozone O

Here, elephant breeding herds have made their home for decades, and Sharpe's Grysbok (page 24) is another unusual, exciting sight.

As in the south, the Ecca Shales form deep soil that can support large trees. The landscape is dominated by large Mopane (page ix) growing to a substantial height of 10-15 m. The rare Arnot's Chat is sought after by Birders, while the Bushveld Bead-bean (*Maerua angolensis*) is conspicuous both when it flowers, from July to October, and when it pods from August through to April.

Mountain Foothills

Three separate mountain ranges border the Lowveld.

- ***The Drakensberg is the most impressive and defines the western and southern edges.***
- ***The Lebombos create the eastern border and are also the international boundary between South Africa and Mozambique.***
- ***The sandstone hills of the Soutpansberg extend into northern Kruger Park, in the Punda Maria-Pafuri area.***

Barberton Daisies (*Gerbera jamesonii*) thrive in rocky, shaded, well-drained positions near Barberton, often on hillsides in the wild.

Drakensberg Mountains

Kiaat Bloodwood (*Pterocarpus angolensis*) is a large striking tree of the western Lowveld.

There are a number of interesting destinations here, including Barberton, Nelspruit, Hazyview and Bosbokrand. The altitude rises to above 550 m. On the lower slopes the rainfall averages 600 mm a year, increasing with altitude. Temperatures are very high in summer (up to 43°C) and drop to single figures in winter – but frost is rare.

The foothills are naturally undulating, being granitic, with different vegetation and animals found in the valleys and on the crests. The transition from the vegetation of the upper foothills – which is Sour Bushveld – to the varied zones of the Lowveld, is very gradual.

In the higher parts of the escarpment, exciting birds such as Long-crested Eagles may be seen, as well as smaller, less conspicuous species such as the Bar-throated Apalis (*Apalis thoracica*). The vegetation in this area includes trees associated with higher rainfall such as the Kiaat Bloodwood (above) and Mobola-plum (*Parinari curatifolia*).

Long-crested Eagle (*Lophaetus occipitalis*) is a small eagle, which often perches on a high vantage point, from where it can spot its prey – rodents and shrews.

Barberton – Nelspruit Mountains

As the Drakensberg mountains sweep southwards, their granitic foothills undulate into Mpumalanga and the west of Swaziland. At 600 m above sea level, Barberton was originally a goldrush town, but now greenstone is mined there (see History page 68 and Grids page 107). Greenstone is our planet's oldest rock, and Barberton is one of very few places in the world where surface outcrops are found. Southern Kruger Park, northern Finland, Greenland, north-eastern Canada, Australia and the Indian Dharwar Craton, are the only other places where it can be seen.

With beautiful scenery and quaint old-world atmosphere, Barberton is more about human history than natural wildlife. Nevertheless, in early summer the hills around the town are covered with white Wild-pear Dombeya flowers (*Dombeya rotundifolia*), and the red flowers of Pride-of-De Kaap Bauhinia (see page xviii). The famous Barberton Daisy (above) is indigenous here, and has been developed into a plant cultivated and grown in gardens worldwide. It was named after Robert Jameson (1832-1919), a German naturalist who brought plants from the district, to be grown in the Durban Botanical Gardens.

The mountains around Barberton are not only beautiful, but they have some of the oldest rocks on Earth.

Malelane Mountains – Ecozone C

The Malelane Mountains are part of the Drakensberg foothills, and create a natural border for the southern end of the Kruger National Park. They are the most mountainous part of the Park with altitudes ranging from 350 to 800 m. They follow the pattern of the rest of the granites, being eroded to relatively gentle undulations. Here, however, the average altitude of each crest is higher, as is the rainfall. The area therefore boasts not only deeper river 'gorges' than the rest of the Lowveld, but also a wide variety of flora and fauna.

Fortunate Birders could see Lazy Cisticola (*Cisticola aberranas*) nearer the mountain tops, while Bushveld Pipit are more common on the lower slopes. A number of special tree species will intrigue Tree Spotters. Along the Nelspruit-Komatipoort road, deciduous Mountain Kirkia will delight you with their striking red foliage in autumn (April and May).

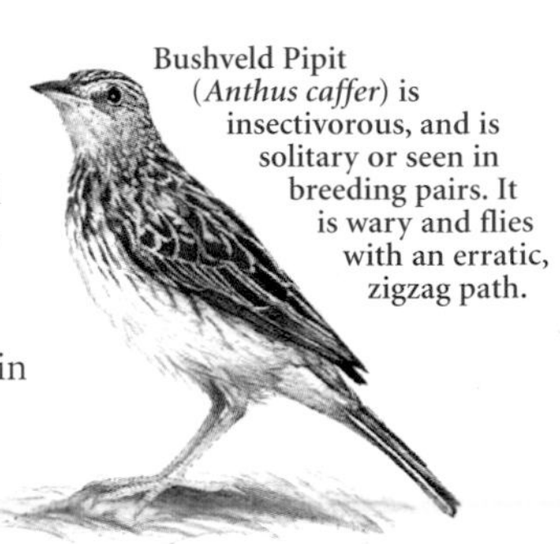

Bushveld Pipit (*Anthus caffer*) is insectivorous, and is solitary or seen in breeding pairs. It is wary and flies with an erratic, zigzag path.

Mountain Kirkia (*Kirkia wilmsii*) are found on the northern slopes of mountains in Ecozone C. The swollen roots have been used as a source of water in dry times.

The Malelane Mountains rise majestically in the west, seen here from near Mpondo Dam in Kruger.

The steeper slopes are the natural home of the Mountain Reedbuck (page 24) and other unusual smaller animals that occur naturally nowhere else in the Lowveld. This includes the Forest Shrew which are voracious predators, hunting during the day but more actively at night. When old enough to accompany their foraging mother, the young form a caravan behind her, each holding on with its teeth near the base of the tail of the one in front.

Forest Shrew (*Myosorex varius*) are endemic to South Africa and Lesotho, and are at the northern end of their range in the Malelane mountains.

Apricot Playboy (*Deudorix dinochares*) fly all year, and are often associated with certain trees which provide larval food through their pods.

Sandstone and Rhyolite

While the Drakensberg Mountains affect the western and southern parts of the Lowveld, two other systems of low mountains or hills also impact on the area – both of them lying inside the Kruger National Park.

The north-western corner of the Park, near Punda Maria, is dominated by sandstone hills and sandveld plains – part of the Waterberg sandstone of the Soutpansberg Mountains (Ecozone N).

Most of the eastern boundary of Kruger is defined by the Lebombo Mountains (Ecozone I) which are also the boundary between South Africa and Mozambique. The base rock is young rhyolite, and the striking red rocks alter the landscape most significantly in the eastern Olifants River area, creating the Olifants Rugged Veld (Ecozone J).

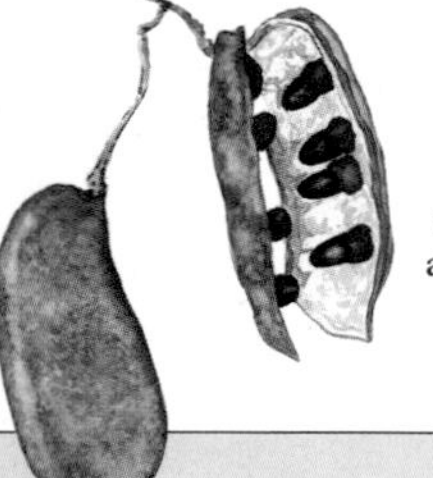

Pod-mahogany (*Afzelia quanzensis*) is one of the Lowveld's grandest trees, and a striking feature of the landscape in Ecozone N.

VAL THOMAS

Baobabs are found throughout the more northerly parts of the Lowveld.

Punda Maria Sandveld –

Ecozone N

Samango Monkeys (*Ceropithecus mitus*) occur only in the extreme north, and are active during the day. They move mainly in trees spending very little time on the ground.

This Sandveld is closely related to the geology of the Soutpansberg. The sandstone ridges are covered by a wide variety of multi-coloured lichens, and in the Nyalaland Wilderness area there are Baobab forests (page i) between the ridges.

The altitude varies between 420 and 580 m, and Punda Maria Sandveld covers an area of about 300 square km. The rainfall is higher than in the surrounding areas, with an annual average of over 500 mm, but the temperatures are generally lower. Many of the special Sandveld trees are found only in this area. Large Pod-mahogony (opposite) are a spectacular feature wherever the landscape is rocky or well drained. Impressive stands of White Kirkia *(Kirkia acuminata)* grow on the sandstone ridges where drainage is sufficient, and they are often out of reach of elephant, that enjoy their soft branches. Animals are relatively scarce in this Sandveld, but some unique bird species such as Broad-billed Rollers may be found during the summer months.

Human history

The far north of the Loweld is a prime area for tourists interested in human history. Numerous old village sites are being restored, where artefacts can be viewed. At both Thulamela and Masorini inside Kruger, there are interesting displays, including an iron smelting site at the latter. These are included in the Grids (page 102).

Broad-billed Roller (*Eurystomus glaucurus*) is an insect-eater. It is an exceptionally striking summer resident in the far north.

LEBOMBO MOUNTAINS – Ecozone I

These volcanic rhyolite mountains run along the eastern boundary of Kruger, from Crocodile Bridge in the south to Shingwedzi in the north. The large eastward flowing rivers – the Olifants, Sabie and Crocodile – cut through them, carving deep gorges. The average altitude of the Lebombos within Kruger varies between 300 and 400 m. The rainfall increases southwards from Shingwedzi, where the average is 400 mm a year, to 700 mm at Crocodile River Bridge.

Surprisingly, waterbuck (page 20) are often found on the rocky slopes, and it is one of the best places to find klipspringer (page 22). The colourful Mocking Cliff-Chat (Mocking Chat) enjoys the rocks, and you may be lucky enough to see a Shelley's Francolin. A variety of Euphorbias (Euphorbia species) contrast with the red rhyolite rocks. Lebombo Euphorbia is one of the rarer trees, as, in Kruger, it occurs only on the Lebombos.

Lebombo Euphorbia (*Euphorbia confinalis*) looks very similar to Bushveld Candelabra Euphorbia (*Euphorbia cooperi*) (page 64). The branchlets in the former have 4 wings, and in the latter, 5-6 wings.

Shelley's Francolin (*Scleroptilia shelleyi*) is one of the rarer francolins. It eats seeds, fruit, bulbs and insects. Its call is a lilting, musical whistle '*I'll-drink-yer-BEER.*'

Euphorbias (left) and White Kirkia (extreme right) are both striking trees in Ecozone J, Olifants Rugged Veld.

Blue-seed Grass (*Tricholaena monachne*) is a pretty, tufted perennial that thrives in the areas with shallow soils in Ecozone J.

OLIFANTS RUGGED VELD – Ecozone J

The open, basalt plains of the south gradually change to the more rugged terrain of the Olifants valley. The rainfall in the area from Satara to the Olifants River is lower than in the south.

Waterbuck and hippo are found all along the river, while zebra and buffalo are the most common grazers.

Purple-pod Cluster-leaf (page 8) and White Kirkia (*Kirkia acuminata*) are trees that both grow on rocky areas and both are easy to recognise.

Shepherds-tree (*Boscia albatrunca*) is a distinctive tree in dry rocky areas, with pale bark and small, tightly packed. leaves.

WATER

Rivers, drainage lines and pans, boreholes and dams provide water for all forms of life. The location of these features affects the distribution of mammals as most of them are dependent upon water.

The associated vegetation forms unique habitats for waterbirds, as well as aquatic animals such as hippos, crocodiles, frogs, terrapins and Monitor Lizards.

Pride-of-De Kaap Bauhinia (*Bauhinia galpinii*) is a spectacular scrambling shrub growing along drainage lines during summer.

RIVERS AND DRAINAGE LINES

Rivers form snaking oases through the often dry landscape. Although many rivers dry up for much of the year, they still provide enough moisture near the surface to ensure essential nourishment for the roots of the riverine trees.

Crowned Hornbills (*Tockus alboterminatus*) are often heard, then seen, flying above rivers. Their call is a plaintive whistle.

Some huge trees grow here. Typical examples are Sycamore Fig (page 11), and Jackal-berry (page 10). Wild Date Palm (page 10) commonly grow in the actual riverbed and provide a home, or refuge, for innumerable water-loving and water-dependent species, as well as cover for stalking predators.

Some animals such as elephant and warthog are able to dig for water when the riverbeds are dry. Deeper pools that form intermittently in the rivers provide water for birds, reptiles, amphibians and fish, even in the dry season.

Riverine vegetation supplies essential shelter and food for many animals. The thicker vegetation is a haven for the shyer creatures such as bushbuck. Birders can look out for the many 'quasi-forest birds' that can be found along the thicker, lush riverine vegetation, including the Purple-crested Turaco (page 51) and various rarer hornbills like the Crowned (above) and Trumpeter (page 50).

Banded Tilapia (*Tilapia sparrmanii*) live in a variety of habitats but generally prefer more stagnant water. The male constructs a nest, and both parents guard their young. They are small, plucky fish that fight agressively, when threatened.

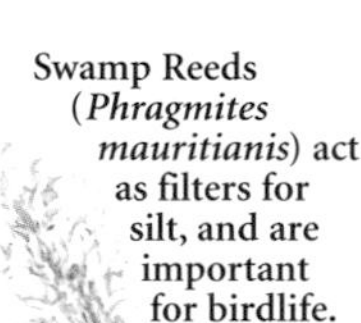

Swamp Reeds (*Phragmites mauritianis*) act as filters for silt, and are important for birdlife.

The scenery around the mighty Olifants River is breathtaking, and the area is rewarding for its prolific sightings of both animal and plant life.

Red-nosed Mudfish (*Labeo rosea*) eat small organisms and algae found on the sandy river bottoms where they live.

Without Pans, animals would not survive in the eastern plains.

Whirligig Beetles (*Dineutus grossus*) swim on the surface of fresh water.

Pans

Pans are another vital water link in the lives of animal populations living or moving nearby. They occur mostly in the flatter areas of the eastern plains, and on the open, sodic (salty clay) areas of the west. They make it possible, during the wet season, for animals to move away from the rivers, where the predators tend to be concentrated. Trees that often grow near the water are Lala Palm (*Hyphaene coriacea*) and Common Spike Thorn. Many sedges (*Cyperus* species), which superficially appear to be stands of tough grass, are found at or near the muddy edges.

Common Spike Thorn (*Gymnosporia buxifolia*) protects itself from browsers with its huge, hard spines.

Dams, Reservoirs and Waterholes

Hippos are frequent sighting in larger rivers and dams (page 19).

Even in the wild, there are man-made structures that help conserve natural water. Dams built across rivers can store large quantities that would otherwise flow past. Windmills or solar-powered pumping units bring underground water to the surface, to fill reservoirs and waterholes.

Throughout the Lowveld, these water-points are created with the intention of providing a stable water supply for animals during dry periods and droughts. They are usually positioned where there were once perennial water sources. This reliable water supply prevents animal losses during severe droughts, and allows the increase in numbers of most of the larger mammal species that attract tourists.

However, it is difficult to anticipate what the effect of such a constant water supply may be. In serious drought conditions – which on past records have occurred in the Lowveld roughly every 30 years or so – it is the lack of food, not water, that causes animals to die in large numbers. The greater the number of animals that survive because of the presence of supplemented water, the more dire the food shortage during drought. Special provision of water may alter the patterns of animal movements seasonally and even year round. This can be detrimental to rare or endangered species. Recent research has shown that waterholes in the north-east of Kruger increased zebra populations in the area. As a result predator numbers increased, and they preyed on the endangered Roan Antelope (page 25). This necessitated the construction of fenced-in, predator-free sections for the breeding of the Roan, in an attempt to improve their chance of survival.

Marsh Terrapins (*Pelomedusa subrufa*) are opportunistic feeders. They remove ticks from wallowing animals. When pans dry out, they bury themselves in mud and hibernate until the rains.

Rocky and Burnt Areas, and Termite Mounds

Rocky outcrops and termite mounds occur sporadically throughout the granite and gabbro of the Lowveld. Both rocks and mounds increase the wide range of habitats, which in turn increases the diversity of plants as well as mammals and birds.

Rocky Areas

Many plants and animals are specifically adapted to thrive in rocky areas.

Leopards often use the koppies to hide and rest, while for baboons they are an ideal vantage point. Nimble klipspringers and dassies, as well as various lizards and insects, are very well adapted to the 'mile-high' life-style.

Higher levels of soil nutrients accumulate amongst the rocks, but water drains away relatively quickly. Therefore, the more drought-resistant Euphorbias (Euphorbia family) and Corkwoods (Myrrh family) grow well here. The long, white roots of Large-leaved Rock Figs, visible on rock faces and plunging down into crevices, are a common but striking sight.

Rock Dassie (Rock Hyrax) (*Procavia capensis*) are only seen in rocky areas, on cool days and moonlit nights, between the Olifants and Bububu rivers.

Fig-tree Blue (*Myrina silenus*) is a beautiful, delicate butterfly. Its larvae feed on wild figs (Ficus species).

Large-leaved Rock Fig (*Ficus abutifolia*) are associated with rocks throughout the Lowveld. The action of their penetrative roots can actually contribute to the splitting of huge boulders.

Burnt areas

Many game species are attracted to the nutrient-rich flush of new green vegetation from recently burnt areas. Zebra in particular, enjoy this artificial spring, and elephant join them as they both relish the toasted ends of twigs!

Fire is an important part of vegetation ecology, and has occurred naturally, at an average interval of 3 to 7 years, for millennia. This has been a major factor in shaping the evolution of plants and, therefore, also of the animals in the Lowveld. However, decisions about managing natural fires and/or burning artificially, are complex. The various authorities and landowners each have their own policies for their territories. Understanding the effect of fire, particularly on herbivores that depend on vegetation for food, is part of the intrigue of the Lowveld game reserves. Be sure to ask for information about the area you are in. There is more information on Fire on page v.

PETER THOMAS

Klipspringer use high rocks as a vantage point for safety from predators.

Termite Mounds (Termitaria)

The large earth mounds seen in the area are usually the homes of the termite *Macrotermes natalensis*. Using chimneys and inlets at ground level, the termites regulate the temperature inside the mounds, within a very narrow range. When you find an active mound, it is easy to feel the hot air rising from a chimney.

This particular species of termite cultivates a fungus garden inside the mound. The fungi break down the cellulose of the termite excrement, making it digestible for both adult and hatchling termites.

Blue Buffalo Grass (*Cenchrus ciliaris*) grows in all types of soil, but prefers sandy or stony areas. Seeds are dispersed by humans.

Termites (*Macrotermes natalensis*) are widespread in southern Africa. These large termites recycle humus and dead wood, but are also well-known wood destroyers.

At dusk, and often after rain, reproductive 'flying-ants' swarm and fly a short distance in vast numbers. They lose their wings, seek a mate, and form a new colony. Often commonly called 'flying-ants', they are not ants at all. The term 'white-ants' for termites is similarly inaccurate.

Numerous animals, from mammals and birds to reptiles, use the mounds as a home or a burrow. Dwarf Mongoose use them for refuge, and the guard animal can often be seen sitting on top of the termitarium. Because of the steady stream of animal occupants, from the initial termites and 'flying-ants' to later home-owners, many predators – bird, mammal, reptile and insect – regularly inspect the area for likely prey.

This is a good example of symbiosis in action. The wide range of activities within the termitarium makes the soil very fertile and moist, enabling easy germination of seeds. The first tree grows easily … then birds on its branches drop more seeds … and small 'tree clusters' develop on and around the mounds. The grass is usually more nutritious than in the immediate surrounding area, and is therefore often cropped visibly shorter, creating a 'ring-road' around the periphery of the mound.

Black Mambas (*Dendroaspis polylepis*) live up to 20 years, are territorial and often make their home in a termite mound. These snakes are lethally poisonous to humans.

DEBORAH WHITE

The raised, sandy top of a termite mound is often a vantage point used by large predators, like this sub-adult lion.

Jacket Plum (page 9) have pale bark and rigid leaves that make them conspicuous amongst other trees growing on old termite mounds.

Plants and Insects

Plants are closely linked to their environment, and reflect changes in climate and soil. This is because plants have evolved over millennia, and adapt to specific soil, temperature and moisture conditions. Common plants found in the Lowveld are susceptible to frost, but can withstand the long, seasonal droughts.

The plants are also adapted to specific patterns of animal usage and to fire. They are all protected in some way against over-usage by browsing animals (page 6). Fire accelerates the breakdown of dead plant material, and encourages new growth.

Because plants provide essential food, as well as nesting and sheltering sites, they determine the different kinds of mammals, birds, reptiles and insects found in an area.

Many insects have been included here as they use the plants in some way, and because they are also associated with specific habitats.

Sizes given refer to the height of the average adult plant, to the wingspan of butterflies, and to the body length of other insects. All trees have been given their national tree numbers. Previous common trees names are given in brackets. The months given after the names of flowering plants refer to the times they flower and bear fruit.

The Ploughbreaker Coral Tree (*Erythrina zeyheri*) is called a suffratex plant – meaning that the main woody stem is actually underground. These plants are called 'Plough-breakers' for a good reason!

PETER THOMAS

Striking and Common Trees

Trees can be identified in a number of ways: by their growth form; by the striking features of leaves, flowers, pods and/or bark; and by the type of habitat/s they prefer. By remembering one or two of the above features, you will learn to recognise common trees.

Wherever you stop, you have a good chance of seeing at least one of the trees on these two pages. Each species has specific habitat preferences, but is more easily recognised by its striking features.

Every tree tells a story about the area in which it grows. By getting to know the trees, you can learn and understand more about the environment as well.

◄▼**Apple-leaf** ▲
Philenoptera violacea
(5 - 18 m) 238
Flowers: Oct - Nov
Pods: Jan - Aug
The irregularly shaped canopy, meandering trunk, and large, pale 3-leaflet leaves are all characteristic. It grows in most parts of the Lowveld, especially along rivers and streams, and most often in groups. Bunches of fragrant, purple flowers appear in summer, and pale brown pods through late summer and the winter.

◄ **African Monarch (Milkweed Butterfly)**
Danaus chrysippus aegyptius
(50 - 70 mm)
The caterpillars feed on the Milkweed (*Gomphocarpus physocarpus*) which contain a toxic, milky latex. The adult butterflies retain this substance, and are poisonous to insect-eaters and are thus avoided. They occur in most habitats.

(M)

Cicada►
Family Cicadidae
(20 mm)
The shrill, monotonous call of male cicadas to attract females is often heard in the bush. They lie up against the trunks of trees, but perfect camouflage makes sightings very difficult.

Knob Thorn ▲► **Acacia**
Acacia nigrescens
(2 - 18 m) 178
Flowers: Jul - Sep
Pods: Dec - May
These upright thorny trees can be identified by the conspicuous woody knobs along the trunks of young trees and larger branches. In spring and early summer, spectacular masses of creamy-white flower spikes cover the canopy. Baboon, monkey and giraffe eat the flowers. White-backed Vultures (page 59) often nest on the tops of the trees.

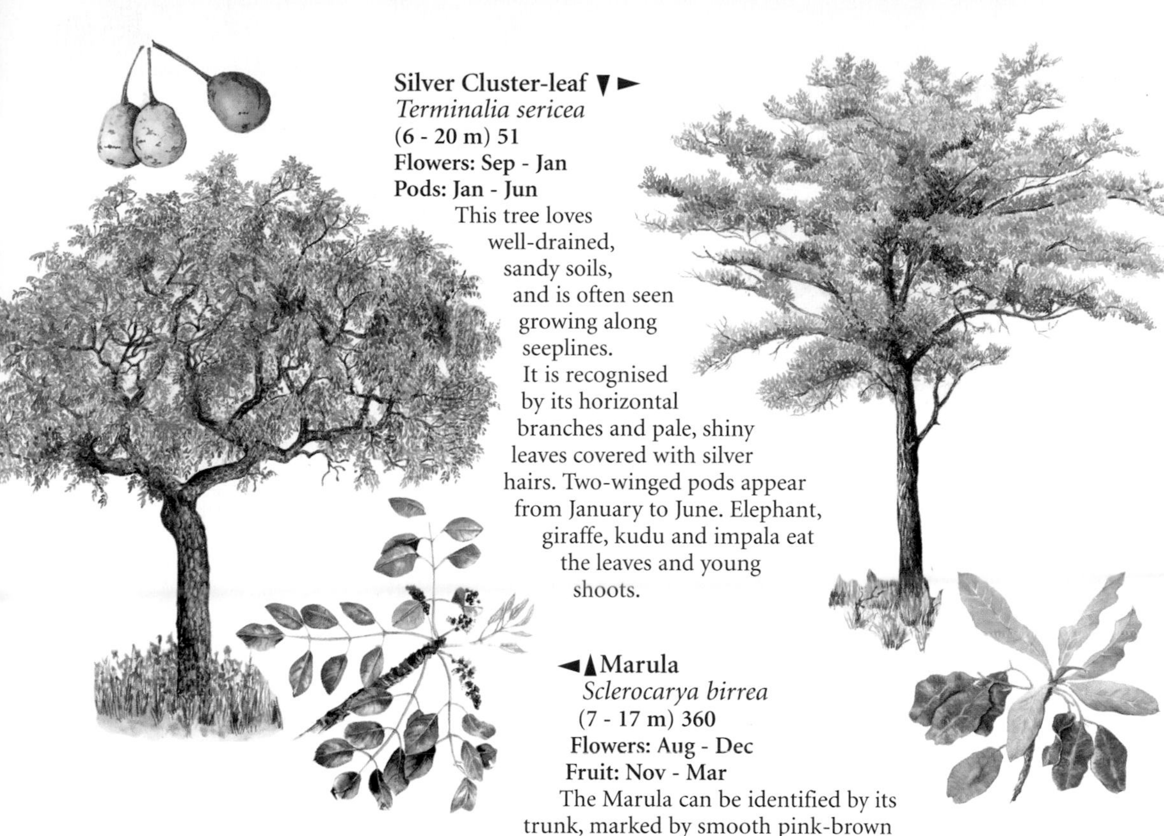

Silver Cluster-leaf ▼►
Terminalia sericea
(6 - 20 m) 51
Flowers: Sep - Jan
Pods: Jan - Jun

This tree loves well-drained, sandy soils, and is often seen growing along seeplines. It is recognised by its horizontal branches and pale, shiny leaves covered with silver hairs. Two-winged pods appear from January to June. Elephant, giraffe, kudu and impala eat the leaves and young shoots.

◄▲Marula
Sclerocarya birrea
(7 - 17 m) 360
Flowers: Aug - Dec
Fruit: Nov - Mar

The Marula can be identified by its trunk, marked by smooth pink-brown depressions lying within dark bark. The tasty fruit, often seen lying under female trees, is eaten by numerous animals, insects, birds and humans. The fruit is used for various products, from jam to a very intoxicating beer. The Marula is one of the most important indigenous fruit-bearing trees. Over hundreds, and even thousands, of years they were at least protected from fire by earlier humans, and later were actually planted. Their presence often indicates ancient settlements in an area.

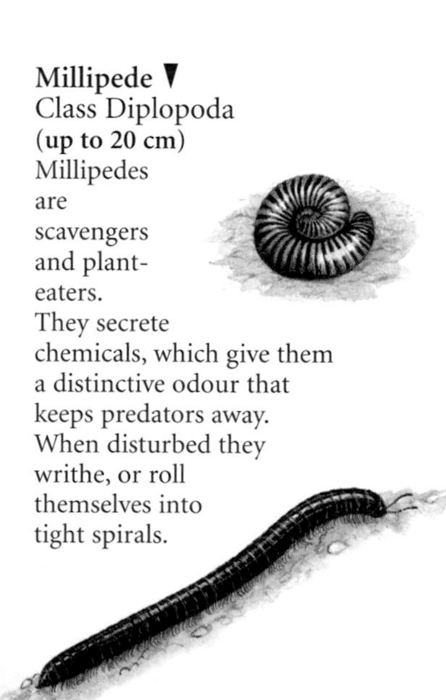

Millipede ▼
Class Diplopoda
(up to 20 cm)
Millipedes are scavengers and plant-eaters. They secrete chemicals, which give them a distinctive odour that keeps predators away. When disturbed they writhe, or roll themselves into tight spirals.

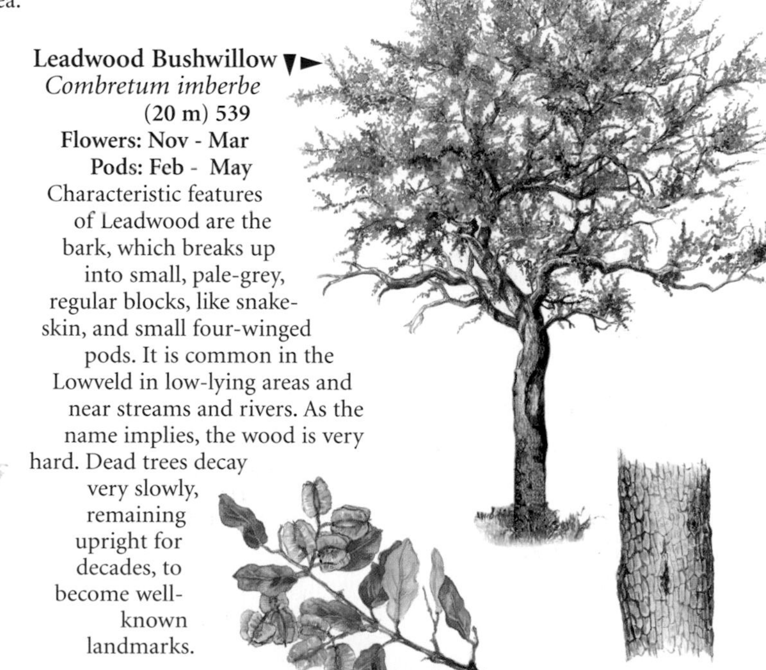

Leadwood Bushwillow ▼►
Combretum imberbe
(20 m) 539
Flowers: Nov - Mar
Pods: Feb - May

Characteristic features of Leadwood are the bark, which breaks up into small, pale-grey, regular blocks, like snake-skin, and small four-winged pods. It is common in the Lowveld in low-lying areas and near streams and rivers. As the name implies, the wood is very hard. Dead trees decay very slowly, remaining upright for decades, to become well-known landmarks.

Trees on the Crests

Tree identification is much easier once you know which common trees you are likely to find in each habitat. The rolling hills of the Lowveld are made up of numerous crests and valleys. The soils of the crests are sandy, and poor in nutrients. Because the soils are infertile, many less tasty, broad-leaved trees grow there, and they tend to be lower in nutrients.

Although these trees are generally unpalatable, their young shoots are a delicacy in spring, and their dropped leaves a supplement in winter. Many of the broad-leaved trees protect themselves by producing various amounts of unpleasant-tasting chemicals. These tannins limit the availability of proteins for the browser by forming unabsorbable compounds. Sometimes animals may be forced to eat these unpalatable plants, which they normally avoid, because no other food is available. Then, because of the high tannin levels, the animals may not absorb enough nutrients for survival.

◄ ▼ **Honey Bee** ►
Apis mellifera adansonii
(15 mm)
These insects have striking colouration to warn predators of their effective defences, and humans are well aware of the Honey Bees' sharp sting. They live in colonies of up to 50 000, and play a vital role in pollination.

◄ **African-wattle** ▲
(African Weeping Wattle)
Peltophorum africanum
(5 - 10 m) 215 Flowers: Sept - Feb; Pods: Dec - Sep
The African-wattle has large, feathery leaves like those of Acacias. It prefers well-drained, sandy soils, and is mostly unpalatable. The abundant yellow flowers are striking, as are the numerous pale pods.

Citrus Swallowtail ▼
Princeps demodocus
(80 - 90 mm)
Males fly around the tops of koppies at midday. Dozens may be seen roosting on grass stems under trees. Their caterpillars feed on citrus trees, and can be a pest in farming areas.

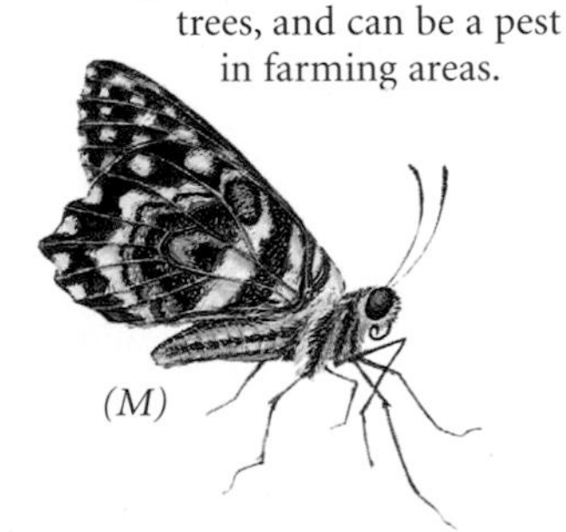
(M)

▲ **Round-leaved Bloodwood** ►
(Round-leaved Teak/Kiaat)
Pterocarpus rotundifolius
(1 - 10 m) 237
Flowers: Sep - Feb
Pods: Nov - Jul
Round-leaved Bloodwood can grow into a tall tree, but in this area is usually seen as a multi-stemmed shrub, having been burnt back by fires. The large, glossy, round leaflets and yellow, pea-shaped flowers are characteristic features. Elephants are fond of the leaves and young twigs, and often break the tree.

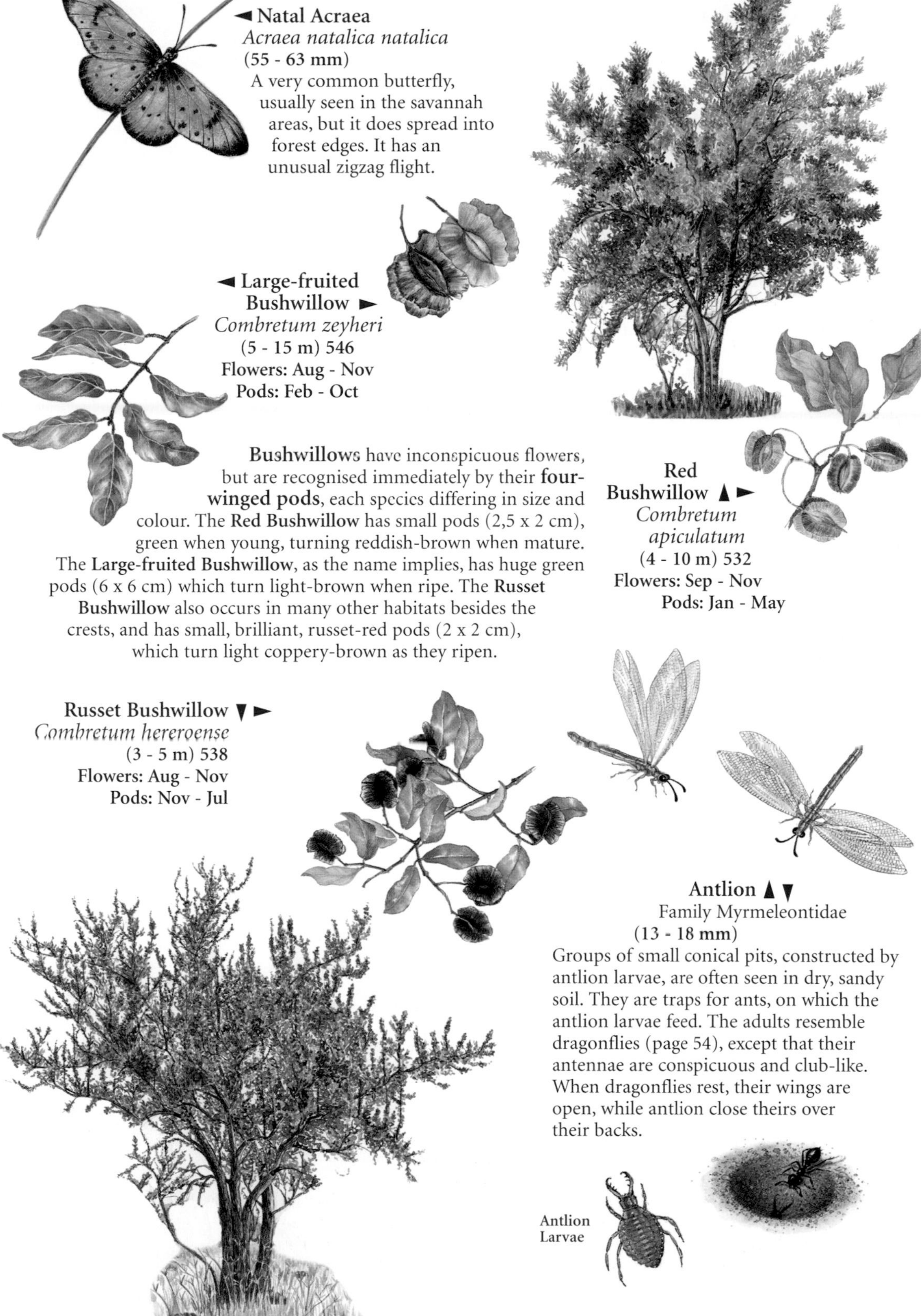

◄ **Natal Acraea**
Acraea natalica natalica
(55 - 63 mm)
A very common butterfly, usually seen in the savannah areas, but it does spread into forest edges. It has an unusual zigzag flight.

◄ **Large-fruited Bushwillow** ►
Combretum zeyheri
(5 - 15 m) 546
Flowers: Aug - Nov
Pods: Feb - Oct

Bushwillows have inconspicuous flowers, but are recognised immediately by their **four-winged pods**, each species differing in size and colour. The **Red Bushwillow** has small pods (2,5 x 2 cm), green when young, turning reddish-brown when mature. The **Large-fruited Bushwillow**, as the name implies, has huge green pods (6 x 6 cm) which turn light-brown when ripe. The **Russet Bushwillow** also occurs in many other habitats besides the crests, and has small, brilliant, russet-red pods (2 x 2 cm), which turn light coppery-brown as they ripen.

Red Bushwillow ▲ ►
Combretum apiculatum
(4 - 10 m) 532
Flowers: Sep - Nov
Pods: Jan - May

Russet Bushwillow ▼ ►
Combretum hereroense
(3 - 5 m) 538
Flowers: Aug - Nov
Pods: Nov - Jul

Antlion ▲ ▼
Family Myrmeleontidae
(13 - 18 mm)
Groups of small conical pits, constructed by antlion larvae, are often seen in dry, sandy soil. They are traps for ants, on which the antlion larvae feed. The adults resemble dragonflies (page 54), except that their antennae are conspicuous and club-like. When dragonflies rest, their wings are open, while antlion close theirs over their backs.

Trees of the Valleys

The vegetation pattern of broad-leaved trees on the crests, and palatable fine-leaved trees in the valleys, can be seen in many of the undulating areas of South Africa. Trees of the valleys are mostly tasty and nutritious, because of the rich, fertile soils in which they grow. They are actively sought by browsing animals. As a result, the trees have had to evolve a variety of defence mechanisms to protect themselves. One obvious defence is the development of thorns or spines to slow down the feeding rate. These may grow all over the plant, from leaf to stem to trunk. Giraffe and Hook-lipped Rhino (page 18), however, have thick, leathery tongues, and are mostly undeterred by thorns on new twigs and branches. Some Acacia trees, being highly nutritious, produce both tannins and thorns.

Some trees form relationships with ants, whereby the ants protect the trees from browsers, and in return receive sugars from the plant.

▲ Buffalo-thorn ►
Ziziphus mucronata
(3 - 10 m) 447
Flowers: Oct - Nov
Fruit: Jan - Aug
The Buffalo-thorn carries its thorns in pairs, one straight and one hooked. The zigzag branchlets and twigs, exceptionally shiny leaves and berry-like fruit are characteristic features. It is the burial tree of the Zulu and Sotho people, and branches are laid on the graves of chiefs and royalty. Hook-lipped Rhino and nyala (page 23) browse the fruit and leaves.

(F)

◄ African Migrant
Catopsilia florella
(40 - 45 mm)
This butterfly is yellow in the wet season and white in the dry season. They often migrate in vast numbers in autumn and summer, and frequently congregate on flowers in summer and autumn.

Sickle-bush ▲ ►
Dichrostachys cinerea
(2 - 6 m) 190
Flowers: Sep - Jan; Pods: May - Sep
Often forming dense thickets, these bushes encroach into open areas, but provide protection for many animals. They are recognised in summer by their flowers resembling Chinese lanterns, and in winter by their very nutritious, tightly coiled pods. Roots, bark, pods and leaves are used medicinally, including treatment for snakebites and toothache.

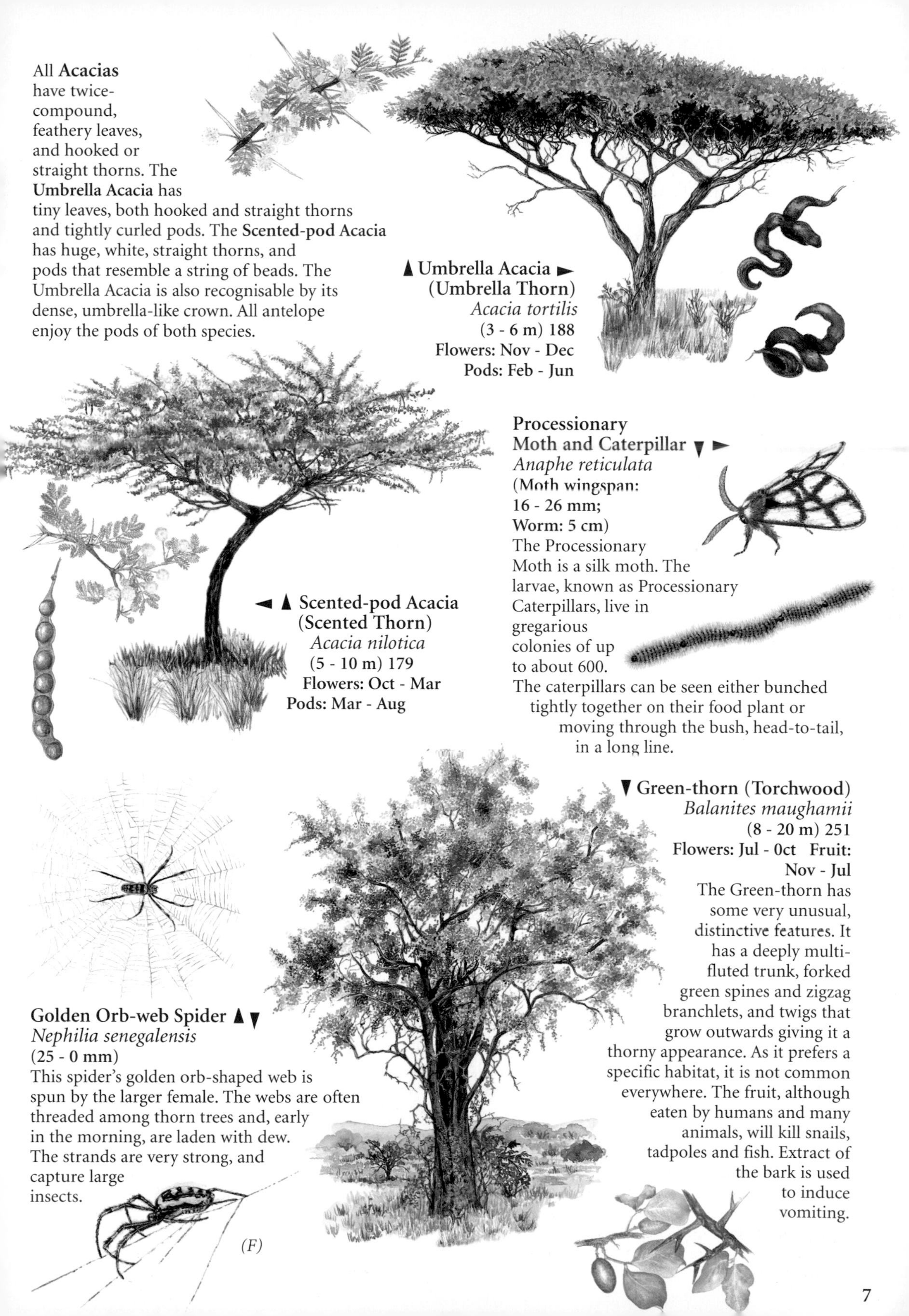

All **Acacias** have twice-compound, feathery leaves, and hooked or straight thorns. The **Umbrella Acacia** has tiny leaves, both hooked and straight thorns and tightly curled pods. The **Scented-pod Acacia** has huge, white, straight thorns, and pods that resemble a string of beads. The Umbrella Acacia is also recognisable by its dense, umbrella-like crown. All antelope enjoy the pods of both species.

▲ Umbrella Acacia ►
(Umbrella Thorn)
Acacia tortilis
(3 - 6 m) 188
Flowers: Nov - Dec
Pods: Feb - Jun

◄ ▲ Scented-pod Acacia
(Scented Thorn)
Acacia nilotica
(5 - 10 m) 179
Flowers: Oct - Mar
Pods: Mar - Aug

Processionary Moth and Caterpillar ▼ ►
Anaphe reticulata
(Moth wingspan: 16 - 26 mm; Worm: 5 cm)
The Processionary Moth is a silk moth. The larvae, known as Processionary Caterpillars, live in gregarious colonies of up to about 600. The caterpillars can be seen either bunched tightly together on their food plant or moving through the bush, head-to-tail, in a long line.

▼ Green-thorn (Torchwood)
Balanites maughamii
(8 - 20 m) 251
Flowers: Jul - 0ct Fruit: Nov - Jul
The Green-thorn has some very unusual, distinctive features. It has a deeply multi-fluted trunk, forked green spines and zigzag branchlets, and twigs that grow outwards giving it a thorny appearance. As it prefers a specific habitat, it is not common everywhere. The fruit, although eaten by humans and many animals, will kill snails, tadpoles and fish. Extract of the bark is used to induce vomiting.

Golden Orb-web Spider ▲ ▼
Nephilia senegalensis
(25 - 0 mm)
This spider's golden orb-shaped web is spun by the larger female. The webs are often threaded among thorn trees and, early in the morning, are laden with dew. The strands are very strong, and capture large insects.

(F)

Trees in Open Areas

Flat open areas have soils that are mostly derived from the erosion of basalt or gabbro rocks. These clay soils are usually high in nutrients. The trees that are easiest to identify are Knob Thorn Acacia and Marula that grow in dense stands (pages 2, 3). Some other trees growing in these open areas, such as the Monkey-orange and Purple-pod Cluster-leaf, are easy to spot because they bear seasonally striking fruit or flowers.

Brackish sites are flat, open patches found along rivers and drainage lines where salts accumulate in the soil. Trees and grasses growing here can tolerate these more salty soils, and are very palatable. Brackish areas can easily be identified by the presence of Magic Guarri.

Purple Tip ►
Colotis ione
(45 - 50 mm)
(M)

These two **Colotis** species can be recognised by the stunning purple and orange tips of their wings. The **Purple Tip** is a fast-flying butterfly that dodges rapidly through open savannah. It is fond of rivers and dry river beds. The **Orange Tip** favours low-lying, hot areas, but avoids woodlands, thickets and slopes. It will fly throughout the year if conditions are right.

◄ **Orange Tip**
Colotis evenina evenina
(40 - 45 mm)
(M)

▼◄ **Black Monkey-orange**
(Hairy Monkey-orange)
Strychnos madagascariensis
(5 - 8 m) 626
Flowers: Nov - Dec
Fruit: All year round

Both these trees are **seasonally striking.** The **Purple-pod Cluster-leaf** has conspicuous purple pods for most of summer, autumn and winter. The hard, green seeds inside the pods are eaten by Brown-headed Parrots, baboons and monkeys. The **Black Monkey-orange** carries orange-sized, green fruit for most of the year, which turns bright yellow when ripe. A range of animals eat various parts of the tree. Humans eat the fruit pulp, but avoid the seeds, which act as a purgative.

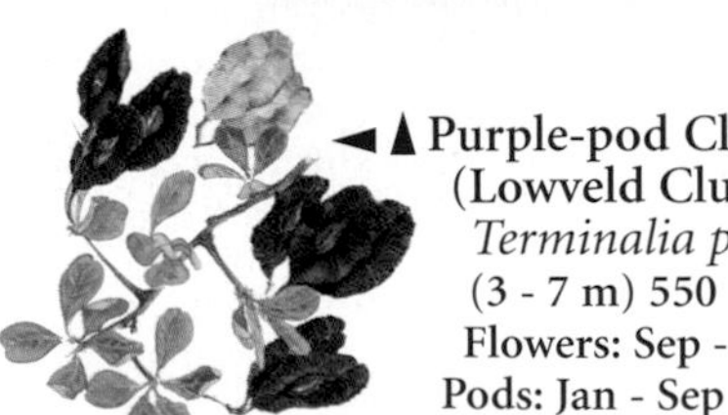

◄▲ **Purple-pod Cluster-leaf**
(Lowveld Cluster-leaf)
Terminalia prunioides
(3 - 7 m) 550
Flowers: Sep - Feb
Pods: Jan - Sep

Bushveld Gardenia ▲►
(Transvaal Gardenia)
Gardenia volkensii
(3 - 10 m) 691
Flowers: Aug - Dec
Fruit: Dec - Aug

▼▲ **Magic Guarri** ►
Euclea divinorum
(4 - 6 m) 595
Flowers: Aug - Sep
Fruit: Oct - Mar

▼**Jacket-plum** *Pappea capensis*
(up to 10 m) 433
Flowers:
Sep - Mar
Fruit:
Dec - Jul

In **brackish flats** the following three trees are common. Characteristics of **Bushveld Gardenia** are the pale-grey bark, large, green, woody fruit and attractive white flowers. The tree was believed to have magical powers and was used to keep evil spirits away. **Magic Guarri** grow in groups, as dense, multi-stemmed bushes with shiny, wavy, leathery leaves. They are unpalatable, and seldom eaten by browsers. The frayed edges of twigs are very effective toothbrushes. **Jacket-plum** has leathery berry-like fruit, which splits open to reveal bright red jelly covering black seeds. The fruit is eaten by a wide variety of mammals and birds, and humans use it to make jelly and vinegar.

(F)

◄ **Brown-veined Migrant**
Belenois aurota
Visible all year (40 - 45 mm)
Favouring open country, this butterfly migrates, south-west to north-east, in late summer in large numbers.

Trees of Rivers and Drainage Lines

The trees that grow along rivers are often the most striking, and by far the largest in the Lowveld. Many have shallow root systems, to prevent the tree from drowning during high-rainfall periods. They are, however vulnerable during drought. If the underground water supply dries up, their roots cannot reach water, and they will die.

The amount of water we use every day affects many other people, as well as the trees and animals that need water to survive. South Africa is a semi-arid country, and water is one of our most precious resources.

◄ ▲ **Jackal-berry**
Diospyros mespiliformis
(10 - 20 m) 606
Flowers: Oct - Dec
Fruit: Jan - Oct
The Jackal-berry has a massive, gnarled or fluted trunk, and trunk-size branches. The leaves are conspicuously wavy, dark green above and paler below. Many animals and birds eat the green berries.

▼ **Wild Date-palm**
Phoenix reclinata
(3 - 6 m) 22
Flowers: Sep - Oct
Fruit: Oct - Jun
This is the only indigenous Lowveld tree with large fern-like leaves and small, date-like fruit. Elephants eat many parts of the tree, while humans eat the fruit, use the sap to brew beer, and weave mats and hats from the leaves. It is found only on riverbanks and in riverbeds.

▲ **Weeping Boer-bean**
Schotia brachypetala; **(15 - 25 m) 202**
Flowers: Aug - Oct; Fruit: Mar - Sep
The canopy of the Weeping Boer-bean curves downwards, and hanging branches may be bare from browsing. It has spectacular dark-crimson flowers in summer. The seeds of the bean-like pods are roasted and eaten.

◄ ▲ **Sycamore Fig**
Ficus sycomorus
(5 - 25 m) 66
Figs: All year round
The massive yellow-pinkish trunk, with smooth bark, peeling in papery sections, makes this tree unmistakable. The masses of clustered figs are eaten by numerous animals and birds. African Green-Pigeons (page 50), Brown-headed Parrots (page 48), hornbills, barbets and rollers, monkeys and baboons relish the fruit.

(M)

◄ **Lowveld Yellow**
Eurema hecabe solifera
Visible all year
(35 - 40 mm)
This butterfly may be seen flying lazily in grass of the Lowveld, but it favours riverine vegetation. The caterpillars feed on Acacias.

Sausage-tree ►
Kigelia africana
(6 - 20 m) 678
Flowers: Jul - Oct
Fruit: All year round
The huge, sausage-like fruit is visible for most of the year, and makes this tree easy to recognise. Not all trees carry fruit. Large, red flowers drip with sweet-smelling nectar, that attracts insects, birds and primates.

(M)

Dancing Acraea ▲
Acraea eponina manjaca
Visible Nov - June
(35 - 40 mm)
This very common butterfly may be seen flying in and out of tall grass at the edges of woodlands and thickets.

◄ ▼ **Tamboti**
Spirostachys africana
(5 - 10 m) 341
Flowers: Jul - Nov; Fruit: Sep - Dec
The rough, dark-brown to black bark, neatly cracked into regular rectangles, is the Tamboti's most striking feature. Broken branches produce a poisonous, extremely irritant, milky latex. Smoke inhaled from fires made from this wood can cause severe illness.

Flowers and Fruit –

Disturbed Areas and Grasslands

After substantial rains a wide variety of flowers can be seen, especially in areas where the grass cover has been removed or disturbed. These flowering plants prepare the bare soil for grasses to re-establish themselves. These pages illustrate the flowers found in disturbed areas (page 14) and in grasslands (page 15).

◄ Wing-seeded Sesame
Sesamum alatum
(up to 1 m) Jan - Mar
Common along roadsides, this tall annual is also found in grasslands. The dry stalks can still be seen during the rainless months. The leaves and roots were formerly used to treat measles, and the seeds are edible.

Yellow Cleome ►
Cleome angustifolia
(up to 1,5 m) Dec - Mar
A non-woody plant (forb), Cleome prefers sandy or rocky soil. It is often the most common flower in disturbed ground, and may cover large areas.

◄ Hammel Stertjie (String of Stars / Wild Heliotrope)
Heliotropium steudneri
(up to 80 cm) Sep - Mar
Masses of the white 'lamb's tail' flowers of this perennial herb may be seen along the roadside during summer. This plant contains an alkaloid that causes liver damage when eaten by animals in large quantities.

▼ Wild Foxglove
Ceratotheca triloba
(up to 2 m) Dec - Feb
This annual will grow in areas where the topsoil has been removed, particularly along roadsides. It has an offensive smell when crushed, and humans apply it to nails to discourage nail-biting.

▼ Wandering Donkey Acraea
Acraea neobule neobule
(45 - 50 mm)
Visible all year
A common species, flying singly all year round, they are often seen around rocky outcrops at midday. The males frequently chase other butterflies.

(M)

▼ Violet
Aptosimum lineare
(5 - 12 cm) Aug - Feb
This small herb grows close to the ground, especially in sandy patches and disturbed areas. It has long, lance-shaped leaves and deep-blue or purple flowers.

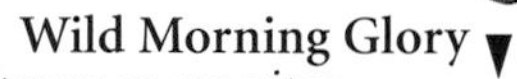

Wild Morning Glory ▼
Ipomoea crassipes
(stems: up to 1 m) Sep - Jan
An erect or trailing perennial, they are often seen hanging from other vegetation or in short grassland in disturbed areas. The roots are eaten raw by humans, and are used as a love potion and to ensure prosperity.

▼ Yellow Pansy
Junonia hierta cebrene
(35 - 40 mm) Visible all year
This attractive butterfly usually flies close to the ground, preferring open ground, grassy spots and gardens. Males can be spotted with their wings open, resting in their territory, which is usually flat, bare ground.

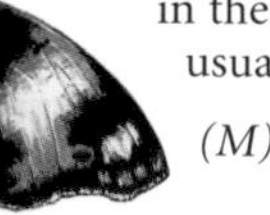

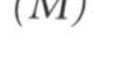
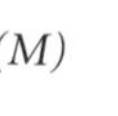

(M)

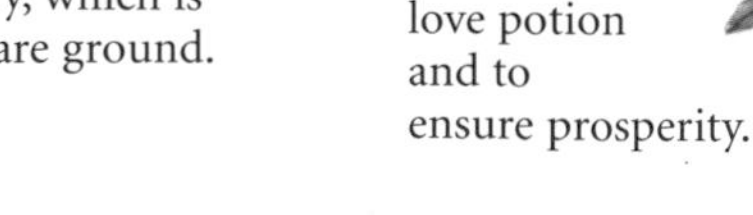

◄ **Impala Lily**
Adenium multiflorum
May - Sep (up to 2 m)
The striking flowers of this succulent shrub are visible in open areas and rocky outcrops. The large, cigar-shaped pods burst open when ripe to release masses of small seeds tufted with long white hairs. All parts contain poisonous milky latex that has been used as a fish poison and on arrow tips.

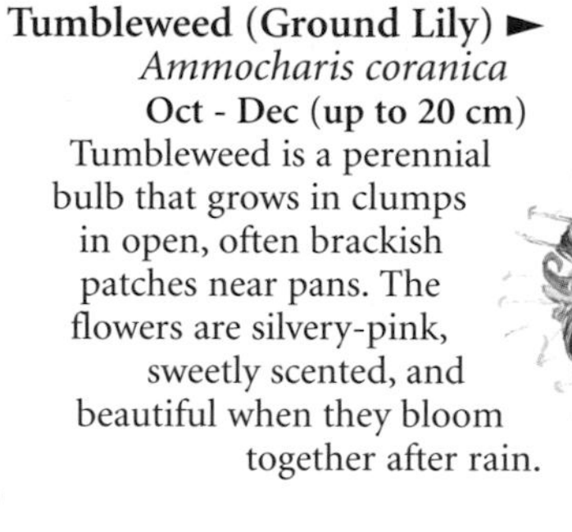

Tumbleweed (Ground Lily) ►
Ammocharis coranica
Oct - Dec (up to 20 cm)
Tumbleweed is a perennial bulb that grows in clumps in open, often brackish patches near pans. The flowers are silvery-pink, sweetly scented, and beautiful when they bloom together after rain.

Vernonia ►
Vernonia fastigiata
Oct - May (up to 1 m)
A bushy, annual herb, its leaves have been used to flavour food.

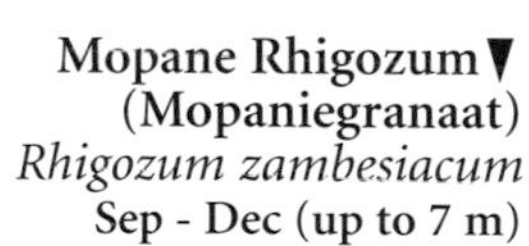

Mopane Rhigozum ▼
(Mopaniegranaat)
Rhigozum zambesiacum
Sep - Dec (up to 7 m)
This spiny shrub is conspicuous when covered in yellow flowers after the first rains. It is most common in brackish sites, in open areas and on rocky hillsides.

◄ **Plakkie**
Cotyledon orbiculata
Mar - Sep (up to 1,5 m)
An evergreen shrub, this Cotyledon may be identified by its succulent, round, grey-green leaves with deep-reddish margins. It prefers to grow on rocky outcrops in grassy slopes. The common name, 'Plakkie', is Afrikaans, meaning to 'place on', from its use as a poultice (a heated leaf) on boils or abscesses.

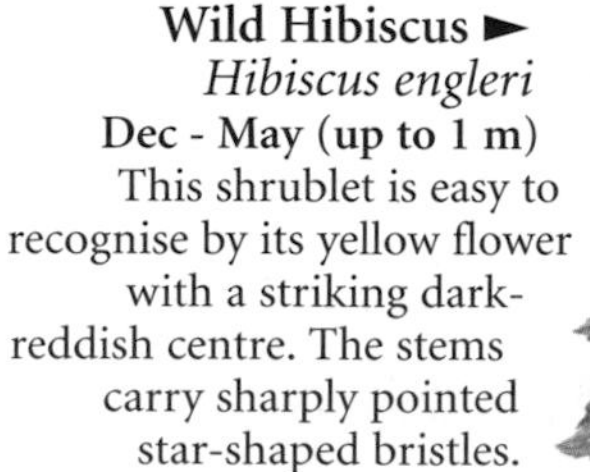

Wild Hibiscus ►
Hibiscus engleri
Dec - May (up to 1 m)
This shrublet is easy to recognise by its yellow flower with a striking dark-reddish centre. The stems carry sharply pointed star-shaped bristles.

Wandering Jew ►
(Blue Commelina)
Commelina erecta
Nov - Feb (20 - 50 cm)
A low-growing, perennial herb with upright or spreading stems. The leaves are narrow, and fold upwards.

Mammals

There is an amazing diversity and abundance of mammal life in the Lowveld. However, only a certain amount of food and habitat space are available. The animals are able to live together and share resources by occupying different niches. Niche separation relates to time (some animals are active during the day, others at night); or to space, (some animals live in open areas, others in a dense habitat). Good examples of this are that cheetah avoid lion and leopard by hunting in open areas during daylight hours, and leopard drag their prey up trees to prevent it being stolen by other carnivores.

The animals have also evolved certain behavioural strategies to help them survive. The herbivorous (plant-eating) mammals may be browsers, or grazers, or both. Browsers usually live in smaller groups in bushy or wooded areas. They either stand completely still or scatter when threatened, using the vegetation as camouflage from predators. Grazers often live on open grassy plains in large groups because many individuals together have a better chance of detecting predators.

Mammals are measured in height
H – ground to shoulder, or in length
L – tip of nose to tip of tail.

On Safari you could have the privilege of counting the spots on the upper jaw of unusually calm leopard. This is the method used to identify different individual leopard.

DEBORAH WHITE

Largest Herbivores

These huge animals consume so much food that they act as modifiers of the landscape. Elephant thin out densely wooded areas, making habitats more suitable for animals such as wildebeest and zebra. Square-lipped Rhino create their own 'grazing lawns', which suit animals like impala but not bushbuck.

A large herd of buffalo can even trample down tall grassland, so that the visibility improves. The grassland then becomes suitable for zebra which previously avoided the area. Hippo change the riverine habitat by eating the surrounding grasses. They also transfer nutrients from adjacent land back into the river, to feed fish and invertebrates. Giraffe shape trees by browsing, and are now thought to pollinate some taller Acacias through pollen transferred on their horns!

All these animals form an important part of an ecosystem, changing the environment enough to make an area more, or less, suitable for a wide variety of species.

◄ **Giraffe**
Giraffa camelopardalis
(H: 3,9 - 5,2 m [M], 3,7 - 4,7 m [F]; 970 - 1 400 kg [M], 700 - 950 kg [F])
The giraffe, the tallest animal in the world, browses in the canopy of trees. Its long, curling tongue and flexible, upper lip are protected by horny papillae for feeding on Acacia trees (pages 2, 7). Despite its height, it has only seven neck vertebrae, the same number as humans. A special system of valves in the neck prevents excessive blood pressure to its head when the giraffe stoops to drink.

Visitors often comment that **rhinos** look prehistoric! As their names imply, the **Hook-lipped Rhino** has a hook-lip, which it uses for browsing, and it is found in dense bush or thickets while the **Square-lipped Rhino** has a square lip, adapted for grazing in open savannah. The calf walks in front of the mother. The Hook-lipped Rhino is slightly smaller, and far more aggressive, and the calf follows behind the mother.

◄ **Hook-lipped (Black) Rhinoceros**
Diceros bicornis
(H: 1,6 - 2,0 m; 800 - 1 100 kg; record horn 1,05 m)

Square-lipped (White) Rhinoceros ►
Ceratotherium simum
(H: 1,8 m; 1 600 - 2 300 kg; record horn 1,58 m)

◄ **Hippopotamus**
Hippopotamus amphibius
(H: 1,5 m; 1 500 kg; tusk-like canines 10 - 30 cm)

These **large, bulk grazers** have totally different lifestyles. **Hippos** spend all day in the water, but at night may cover many kilometres feeding on short grass. They are gregarious, living in pods of about 15, which include dominant bulls. It is very dangerous to be between a hippo and the water. Their huge bulk may appear slow, but they are exceptionally fast on land. **Buffalo** prefer the open savannah with tall, coarse grass for feeding. They live in herds of up to 500, although old, solitary bulls are often seen. A buffalo will raise its nose into the air to try to catch the scent of a predator. Old, hot-tempered bulls can charge unexpectedly, and the buffalo is therefore considered one of Africa's most dangerous species.

▲ **Buffalo**
Syncerus caffer
(H: 1,6 m; 750 kg; record horn 1,29 m)

Elephant ►
Loxodonta africana
(H: 3,2 - 4,0 m [M], 2,5 - 3,4 m [F]; 5 000 - 6 300 kg [M], 2 800 - 3 500 kg [F]; record tusk 102,3 kg)

Elephants live in stable, social units led by a matriarch. Mature bulls form bachelor groups, or are seen wandering alone. The elephant uses its highly dexterous trunk in every aspect of its life, from drinking and feeding to communication. It flaps its large ears, rich in blood vessels, to get rid of excess heat. Elephants are generally peaceful animals, but can become extremely aggressive if harassed, threatened or sick.

▼ **Koppie Charaxes**
Charaxes jasius saturnus
(75 - 100 mm)

Charaxes species are often seen sucking fluid from elephant dung, or the sap of damaged trees. Males of the Koppie Charaxes often visit the tops of ridges and koppies at midday. The caterpillar's food includes Boer-bean species (page 10).

(F)

GRAZERS

Animals that prefer open areas are usually grazers, and they tend to congregate in large groups. Visibility is very important, as their best defence is to spot predators early enough to be able to escape. The main predators here are lion and cheetah. Grazers share available grasses by using different parts of the grass layer, or choosing different types of grass. Some species eat selectively, such as Common Reedbuck, while others, such as zebra, feed on a wide range of grasses. This means that there is more food to go around, and less competition.

Some herbivores, such as zebra and wildebeest, establish beneficial relationships with one another. Their feeding habits are complementary, and because they graze together, there are more eyes and ears to warn against stalking predators.

The interactions between plants, animals and the environment are interdependent. Each species plays an invaluable role in the survival of the whole system.

Warthog ▼
Phacochoerus aethiopicus
(H: 70 cm; 60 - 100 kg; tusks 12 cm [M], 3 cm [F])
Warthogs, named for their facial warts, live in family groups. They have poor eyesight, and may approach quite close to visitors, rooting about on their knees. When disturbed, they spend a few seconds staring, then run off with tails held erect. They shelter at night in holes in old termite mounds burrowed out by aardvark (page 33).

Bushpig ►
Potamochoerus porcus
(H: 60 - 85 cm; 35 - 60 kg; tusk-like canines 5,6 cm [M], 4,5 cm [F])
Bushpigs are nocturnal and very secretive, and few visitors are lucky enough to spot them. The best place to see one is on a nightdrive, or in the dense riverine bush between the Luvuvhu and Limpopo rivers.

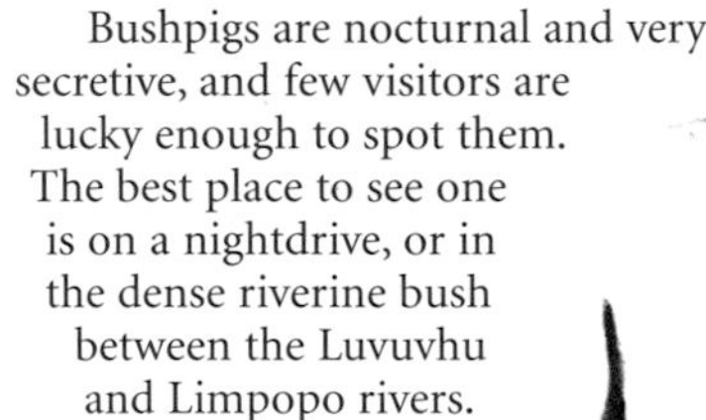

◄ Waterbuck ►
Kobus ellipsiprymnus
(H: 1,7 m [M], 1,3 m [F]; 260 kg [M], 230 kg [F]; horn 75 cm)
Lyre-shaped, forward-pointing horns, and the white ring around the rump, make the waterbuck unmistakable. When pursued, it often takes refuge in water, and swims readily. Waterbuck live in small herds, in tall-to-medium grass and hilly areas, close to water.

(M)

(M)

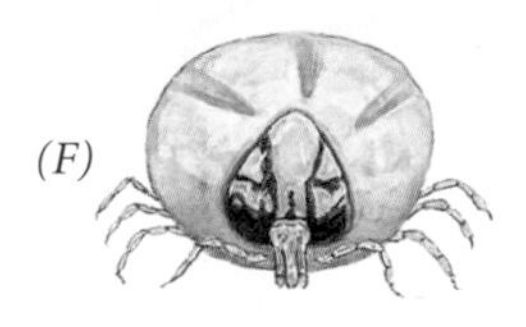

Blue Tick ▼▲►
(Bontbosluis)
Amblyoma hebreaum
(3 - 12 mm)
The tick larvae are called pepper ticks because of their minute size. When the eggs hatch on the ground, the larvae crawl up and hang in clusters (2 000 - 20 000) at the ends of vegetation, waiting for a host to pass by. All ticks transmit human and animal diseases, such as tick-bite fever. This tick transmits heart-water in cattle, but wild animals are not susceptible. In tick-infested areas, visitors should examine themselves regularly, and remove any ticks found on the skin.

Larvae
(pepper-grain size)

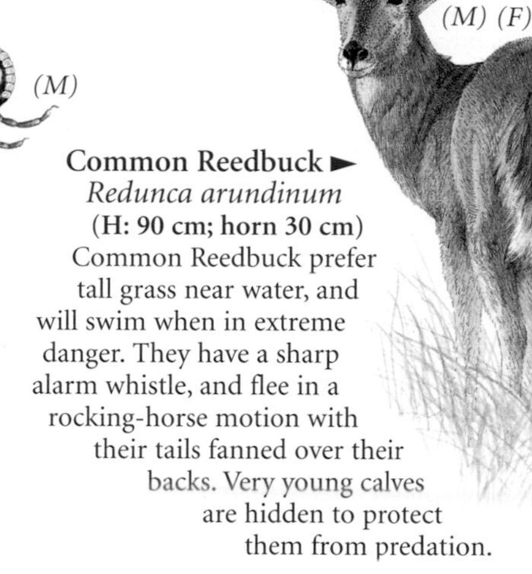

Common Reedbuck ►
Redunca arundinum
(H: 90 cm; horn 30 cm)
Common Reedbuck prefer tall grass near water, and will swim when in extreme danger. They have a sharp alarm whistle, and flee in a rocking-horse motion with their tails fanned over their backs. Very young calves are hidden to protect them from predation.

◄ Dung Beetle
Family
Scarabaeidae
(5 - 50 mm)
Dung Beetles are often seen rolling fresh dung into balls. An egg is laid inside the ball, which the beetle may bury underground. They clean up decaying matter and carry nutrients underground, playing an important role in the ecosystem.

◄ Plains Zebra
(Burchell's Zebra)
Equus burchelli
(H: 1,3 m; 290 - 340 kg)

Zebra and Blue Wildebeest are both **highly gregarious herd animals**, breeding in spring and summer. **Zebra** feed on taller grass, and often graze together with **wildebeest**, which prefer short grass. Both wildebeest and zebra rely on each other's eyesight and alertness. In addition, the zebra's stripes confuse predators: when the herd bunches together it appears to be a single unit.

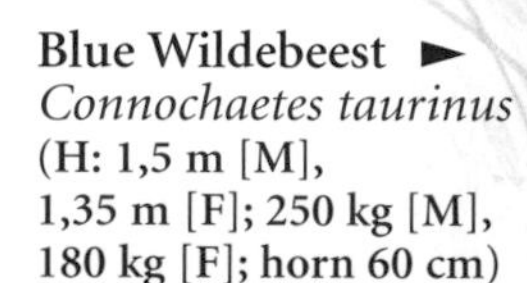

Blue Wildebeest ►
Connochaetes taurinus
(H: 1,5 m [M], 1,35 m [F]; 250 kg [M], 180 kg [F]; horn 60 cm)

Browsers

The savannah areas, which are covered with trees, provide shelter and food for many species, especially browsers. Many browsers have narrow muzzles to pick the fine, nutritious leaves off Acacia trees (pages 2, 7). Trees have deterrent chemicals (tannins) designed to reduce excessive browsing. Browsers have themselves adapted to avoid eating large amounts of tannin (page 4).

Like grazers, different species of browser eat different parts of the vegetation, which means that there is more food available to a variety of animals. Giraffe feed from the top parts of the canopy, kudu in the middle, while smaller antelope like steenbok, feed only on small bushes or trees. Elephant eat at every level, and often include bark, pods and fruit in their diet.

The different types of vegetation on crests and valleys provide animals with the opportunity to choose the most palatable diet each season. The fresh, green grass on crests in summer gives the grasses in the valleys a chance to recover from winter grazing.

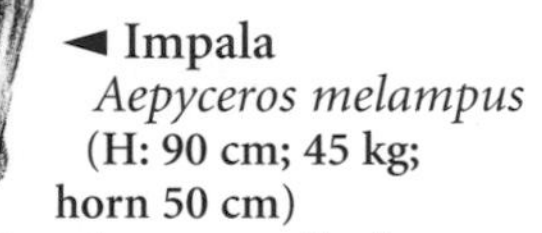

◄ **Impala**
Aepyceros melampus
(H: 90 cm; 45 kg; horn 50 cm)

Impala are usually the most common antelope, browsing and grazing in variable size herds of up to 100. When alarmed they 'blow' or 'snort'. While running, they confuse predators with enormous leaps of up to 3 metres high and 11 metres long. At mating time, around April and May, the snorting and grunting of rutting males can be heard over great distances.

▲ **Steenbok**
Raphicerus campestris
(H: 50 cm; 11 kg; horn 9 cm)

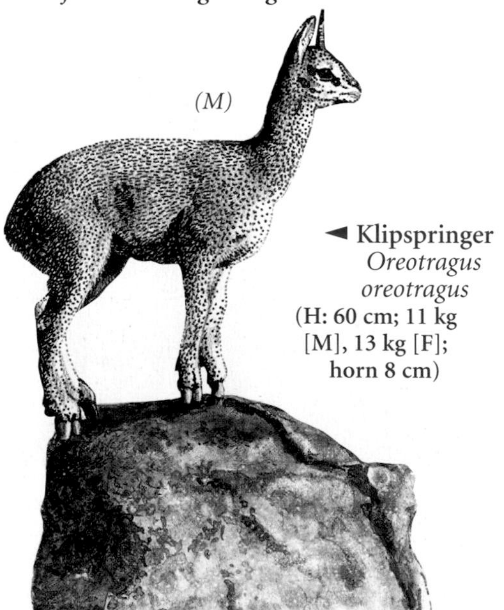

◄ **Klipspringer**
Oreotragus oreotragus
(H: 60 cm; 11 kg [M], 13 kg [F]; horn 8 cm)

It is not difficult to distinguish between these three **small browsers.** The **steenbok** live in the plains or open savannah. **Klipspringer** are very territorial, and inhabit rocky hills or koppies. Both these species obtain most of their water from juicy plants, and are therefore unusual in not being dependent on water.

The **Common Duiker** (opposite page) is found in the undergrowth and thickets along watercourses, browsing leaves, fruit, flowers and seeds. Both the duiker and the steenbok are mostly solitary, except when breeding. Klipspringer live in pairs or small family groups.

Kudu ►
Tragelaphus strepsiceros
**(H: 1,4 - 1,5 m;
250 kg [M],
180 kg [F];
horn 1,2 m)**

These three antelope are **large browsers**. They live in small groups, and may appear similar. **Kudu**, however, frequent dense savannah and hilly terrain, while **nyala** move around riverine bush. Kudu males have long spiralled horns, and although the horns of nyala males also twist, they are shorter. Kudu are extremely agile, and can jump 2-metre-high fences from a standing position. Both species bark when alarmed.

Bushbuck are even smaller than nyala, and the males' horns are straighter. They have stripes along their sides like the others, but may also be recognised by the white spots on their flanks. They are often seen alone, near rivers, but are shy and secretive and move about in the thickets and dense undergrowth.

Bushbuck ▼
Tragelaphus scriptus
(H: 70 - 80 cm; 45 kg [M], 30 kg [F]; horn 26 cm)

Nyala ▲
Tragelaphus angasii
**(H: 1,1 m [M], 1 m [F];
110 kg [M], 60 kg [F]; horn 60 cm)**

◄ Common Duiker
Sylvicapra grimmia
**(H: 50 cm; 18 kg [M],
21 kg [F]; horn 11 cm)**

Rare, Specialised Antelope

These antelope have very particular habitat requirements, and spotting one of them is a special bonus. Roan prefer the open grasslands bordering seasonal rivers, while tsessebe can often be seen close to water points. The best chance of sighting them is on the basalt plains north of the Shingwedzi River, although some individuals may be found north of the Olifants River. Sable Antelope prefer the more wooded areas on the granites, while Sharpe's Grysbok prefer hilly areas or thickets along drainage lines in the north.

The interactions between plants, the mammals and smaller animals that are associated in their particular habitat, are totally interdependant. The rare Yellow-billed Oxpecker, the very common Cattle Egret, and the rare fascinating Rhinoceros Beetle are all part of the endless cycle.

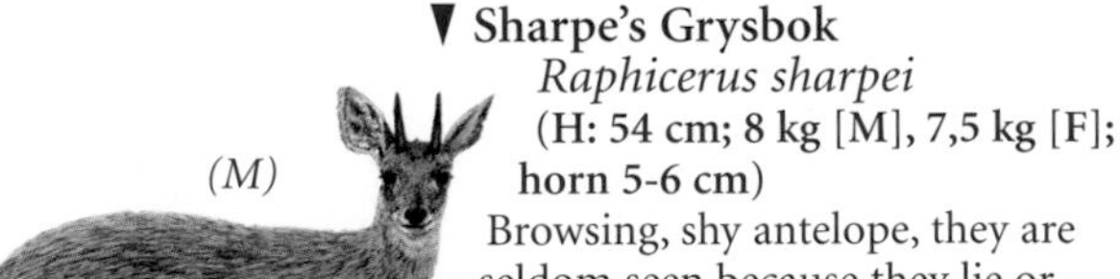

▼ Sharpe's Grysbok
Raphicerus sharpei
(H: 54 cm; 8 kg [M], 7,5 kg [F]; horn 5-6 cm)
Browsing, shy antelope, they are seldom seen because they lie or stand very still, when afraid. They are active at night, and normally on their own but can be found in the daytime in dense thickets along rivers or on hills, particularly in the sandstone of the far north.

(M)

Mountain Reedbuck ►
Redunca fulvorufula
(H: 70 - 75 cm; 30 kg [M], 28 kg [F]; horn length 20-25cm)
These antelope are grazers, found in the Malelane mountain area in the Lowveld. Although they are seldom seen, their shrill nasal whistle can alert you to their presence. They occur in herds of 3 - 6, and may be confused with the Common Reedbuck (page 21) which prefers the tall grass along rivers. Mountain Reedbuck have reddish heads and necks. Only the males have horns and these curve forward.

◄ Yellow-billed Oxpecker
Buphagus africanus
(22 - 23 cm) 771
This exteremely rare, tick-eating bird is very similar to the Red-billed Oxpecker (page 46). Recorded as extinct in South Africa a few years ago, it was successfully re-introduced into Umfolozi-Hluhluwe Reserves, and now naturally occurs in the Lowveld too. It plucks insects off the host mammals, especially giraffe. The Red-billed has a reddish bill and brown rump, and the Yellow-billed has a pale rump.

Cattle Egret ►
Bubulcus ibis
(54 cm) 71
These birds are often found in large numbers, in association with grazing animals. This is because they feed on the insects disturbed by the moving herd. They fly in large V-formation to and from their communal roosts in reed beds.

(M)

◄ Tsessebe
Damaliscus lunatus
(H: 1,2 m; 140 kg [M], 120 kg [F]; horn 34 cm)
The population of these grazing antelope has declined severely following the drought in the early 1990s, and it is a rare privilege to sight one of them. They prefer open grassland areas, and can be seen naturally, in the northern basalts of Kruger. Tsessebe herds are very stable and cows do not move between herds.

Mopane Moth ▲
Imbras belina
Other than occasional sightings, the rare antelope on this page are generally found further north in the Lowveld, where the vegetation is predominantly Mopane (*Colophospermum mopane*). Wherever these Mopane trees grow, there are Mopane Worms and Moths.

Eland ►
Taurotragus oryx
(H: 1,7 m; 700 kg; horn 0.8 m;)
Eland are the largest of the antelope, and can cross ordinary game fences quite easily. Able to browse and graze, they cover great distances. Herds or single bulls may be seen north of the Olifants River. When browsing, they break bushes with their horns to reach the soft, green growth points.

(M)

(M)

◄ Sable Antelope
Hippotragus niger
(H: 1,35 m; 250 kg [M], 210 kg [F]; horn 1 m)
Although Sable numbers have also dropped after the droughts of the '90s, their population is still healthy. They prefer wooded areas, and are more common in the granites. They are one of the most striking antelope on Earth. Bulls are almost black, while females have much browner coats. Their scimitar-shaped horns are formidable weapons against predators.

Rhinoceros Beetle ▼
Oryctes boas **(30 mm)**
The male beetles have a horn which they use in fights with other males The larvae, large white grubs, are often found in decomposing vegetation or animal dung.

(M)

Roan Antelope ►
Hippotragus equinus
(H: 1,55 m, [M],1,45 m [F]; 280 kg [M], 250 kg [F]; horn 75 cm)
A critically threatened species, there are very few breeding herds of Roan in the Lowveld, and most of these are on the basalts, north of the Shingwedzi River. In an attempt to increase numbers and stabilise the population, two Roan breeding camps have been established near Mopane and Punda Maria in Kruger Park. These antelope have very specific social requirements, and adult cows play a significant role in the selection of foraging areas and in keeping a lookout for predators.

Larger Carnivores

These large hunters have always fascinated humans, perhaps because we are basically hunters too. Carnivores are at the top of the food chain in the wild, preying on herbivores. They are well adapted for hunting, with excellent eyesight and hearing, sharp teeth, and bodies designed for speed and/or power. Scavengers have an acute sense of smell to help them locate dead carcasses. Their teeth and jaws are exceptionally powerful for grinding bones.

All predators are opportunistic, seizing the easiest chances to catch prey. They eliminate the old, sick and weak animals first, while the strongest and fittest survive. Predators therefore play an important role in the ecosystem, helping to maintain strong, healthy herbivore populations.

Humans are not perceived as being natural prey. However, a sudden movement, standing up, or a loud noise can create a potentially dangerous situation in an open landrover or on foot.

◄ Wild Dog
Lycaon pictus
(H: 68 cm; 24 - 30 kg)
The Wild Dog is diurnal, and is an endangered species. Wild Dogs are highly co-operative, hunting and breeding in packs of up to 40 animals. Wild Dogs don't conceal themselves when hunting. They chase their prey for several kilometres to the point of exhaustion. One dog may grab the prey by the muzzle, allowing the other dogs to disembowel it. The pack is headed by one breeding pair, but the other members help to look after and feed the young.

Black-backed Jackal ►
Canis mesomelas
(H: 38 cm; 6 - 10 kg)

Side-striped Jackal ▼
Canis adustus
(H: 40 cm; 8 - 10 kg)

These **two species of jackal** are not really direct competitors. The **Black-backed Jackal** favours more open savannah grassland. The **Side-striped Jackal** prefers thickly wooded country, is more strictly nocturnal, and less often seen. Jackals are efficient hunters, killing whatever is available – young antelope, rodents, hares, birds, reptiles, fish and insects, and both species will scavenge readily, following predators. They also eat fruit and berries as we see from the common riverine tree named Jackal-berry (page 10). In both species, pairs mate for life.

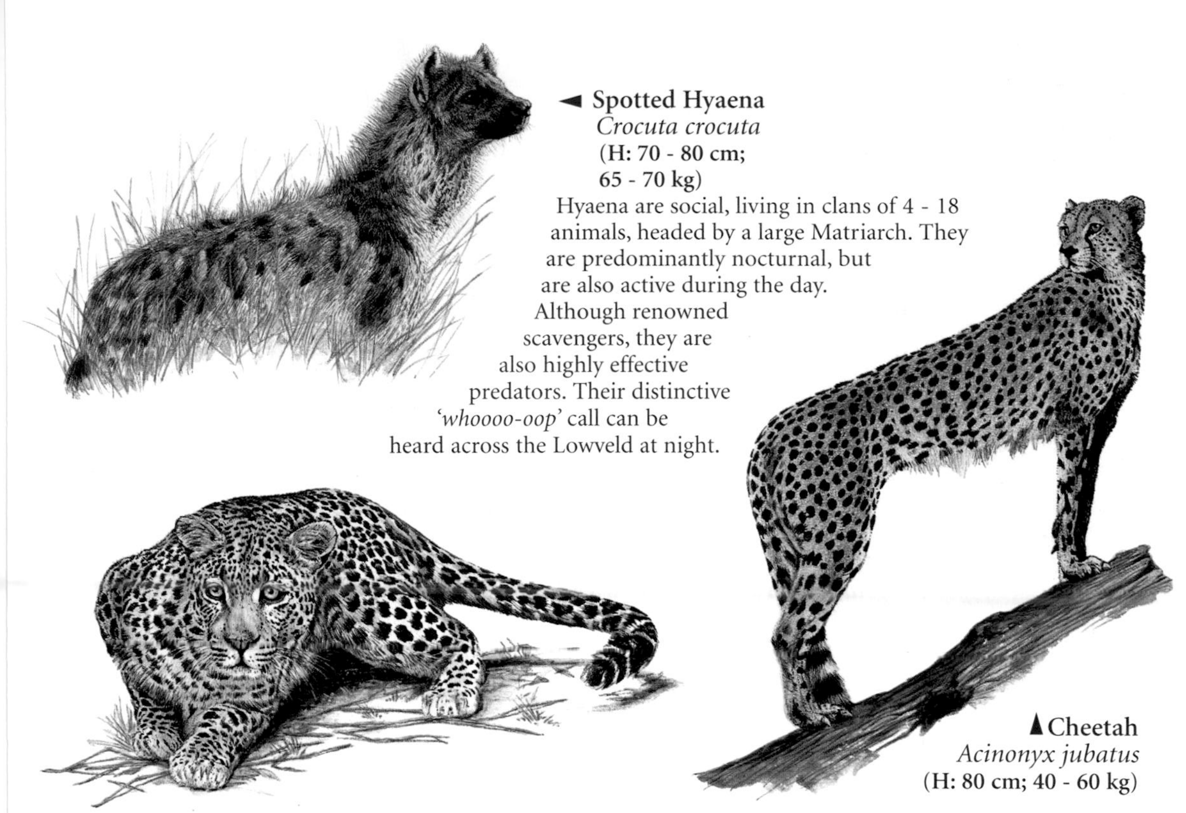

◄ **Spotted Hyaena**
Crocuta crocuta
**(H: 70 - 80 cm;
65 - 70 kg)**

Hyaena are social, living in clans of 4 - 18 animals, headed by a large Matriarch. They are predominantly nocturnal, but are also active during the day. Although renowned scavengers, they are also highly effective predators. Their distinctive '*whoooo-oop*' call can be heard across the Lowveld at night.

▲**Cheetah**
Acinonyx jubatus
(H: 80 cm; 40 - 60 kg)

Leopard ▲
Panthera pardus
**(H: 70 - 80 cm;
40 - 70 kg)**

These three **large carnivores** have different lifestyles. The **leopard** is a solitary and secretive animal. It spends most of its day in hiding. It hunts by ambushing its prey, and lives in dense bush, forest or rocky areas. **Cheetah** need open areas to hunt, as they rely on speed to catch their prey. They are the fastest land mammal on Earth, with estimated top speed of about 100 km/h. They are often solitary but some males form small coalitions, and females are often seen with their young. **Lions** are social animals that observe a strict hierarchy within the pride. Although lionesses do most of the hunting, males that are present feed first, followed by females and cubs. When food is scarce, cubs cannot compete with adults, and 80% of cubs born may starve to death. Lions require some concealment for stalking, then cover the final distance in a fast charge.

(F)

A type of carnivore hierarchy exists in the savannah, depending on the size and strength of the animal and its group. Lions are usually the dominant predator, and may inflict serious losses on cheetah and Wild Dog populations sharing the same habitat.

(M) *(F)*

◄ **Lion** ►
Panthera leo
**(H: 1 m;
180 - 230 kg [M],
113 - 160 kg [F])**

Smaller Mammals

There are a number of other interesting mammals in the Lowveld that are not part of the larger carnivore and herbivore groups. They are mostly omnivorous, feeding on both plant and animal life. They too fill a specific niche within the environment, and have particular behavioural strategies best suited for survival.

One of the most interesting aspects of these creatures is the co-operation between species. Dwarf Mongooses often live in active termite mounds, where they favour the cooler temperatures found inside. They often hunt with hornbills (page 45), which catch any insects the mongoose might disturb. In return the hornbills may warn the smaller mammals if any danger is approaching, such as an eagle.

Many of the smaller species cannot afford to be particular about their food choice, especially when resources are limited. These less specialised species often have a wide distribution, and survive better during hard times because of this adaptability.

◄ **Tree Squirrel**
Paraxerus cepapi
(L: 34 cm; 190 g)
Tree Squirrels live in small family groups, but forage on their own for fruit seeds, shoots, roots and insects. They are highly vocal, communicating with each other using a variety of calls. Group members share a nest and carry the same smell. Strangers lacking the family smell are chased off.

▼ **Common Molerat**
Cryptomys hottentotus
(L: 16 - 18 cm; 153 g)
As with true moles, the presence of these rodents is revealed by the mounds of earth thrown up as they excavate their tunnels. They eat corms and tubers, and therefore perform an important function in plant dispersal. Tubers may be carried for distances of over 60 m.

▼ **Banded Mongoose**
Mungos mungo (L: 60 cm, 1,4 kg)

Mongooses are all **insectivorous,** but include things like bird and reptile eggs in their diet. There are eight species in the Lowveld, and three are shown here (and White-tailed on page 28). The **Banded Mongoose** lives in dense savannah in thickets and on rocky outcrops. The **Slender Mongoose** is solitary, often seen along the roadside, hunting rodents, reptiles, birds and insects. The **Dwarf Mongoose** prefers open savannah with termitaria or other hiding places. Both the Dwarf and Banded Mongoose are highly social, living in large groups of up to 30 animals. Birds of prey (pages 58, 59) are the main enemies of mongooses.

Slender Mongoose ▼
Galerella sanguinea
(L: 58 cm; 710 g [M], 570 g [F])

Dwarf Mongoose ▲
Helogale parvula
(L: 38 cm, 260 g)

Both Vervet Monkey and Chacma Baboon are **social and omnivorous primates**, but live in different habitats and behave differently. **Vervet Monkeys** are more common than baboons, and spend their time in the trees near rivers, using them for food, shelter and refuge. **Baboons** are ground-based, ranging across a variety of habitats. They need rocky hills or habitats with tall trees for sleeping, finding refuge and posting sentries. The leopard (page 27) is their main predator.

▼ Chacma Baboon
Papio ursinus
(L: 1,35 m; 30 kg [M], 16 kg [F])

Vervet Monkey ▲
Cercopithecus aethiops
(L: 1 m; 5 kg)

▼ Honey Badger
Mellivora capensis **(L: 95 cm; 12 kg)**
Generally solitary, the Honey Badger feeds on rodents, reptiles, insects, larvae of Dung Beetles (page 21), eggs, ground birds, wild fruit and honey. It is exceptionally strong, and uses its long, sharp claws to dig for prey or to make a hole for sleeping and breeding. Honey Badgers are formidable fighters and predators, protecting themselves with courage and ferocity.

Cape Clawless Otter ▼
Aonyx capensis **(L: 1 - 1,3 m)**
Although these animals are quite common in the larger perennial rivers of the Lowveld, they are very seldom seen because they are active from late afternoon to early morning. They feed on fish, crabs and freshwater mussels, and their foraging areas can often be identified by their dung and the remains of their prey.

Nocturnal Animals

These fascinating nocturnal mammals fill a different niche in the night-life world, feeding on plants and insects. They often fall prey to carnivores, and defend themselves in diverse ways. Porcupines walk backwards rattling their sharp quills, while bushbabies leap about in tree canopies. The Scrub Hares lie in the grass with their big ears flattened against their heads. All these animals are part of the food chain that keeps the system alive.

Night-life offers another world of experience, full of new sounds, smells and excitement. A wandering spotlight will pick out the shining eyes of animals actively going about their nocturnal business.

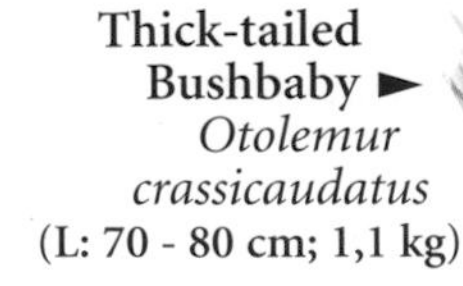

Thick-tailed Bushbaby ►
Otolemur crassicaudatus
(L: 70 - 80 cm; 1,1 kg)

Bushbabies **live in trees, and are very agile**, leaping 2 - 3 metres across branches. They wipe urine on their feet and hands to scent-mark their territory. Bushbabies are preyed on by genets (page 28) and owls (page 60, 61). They forage alone for gum, fruit and insects, but sleep in the daytime in family groups. The **Thick-tailed Bushbaby** lives in well-wooded areas, while the **Lesser Bushbaby** prefers the savannah (especially Acacia). The Thick-tailed Bushbaby has a call like a crying baby, hence its name.

▲ Lesser Bushbaby
Galago moholi
(L: 30 - 40 cm; 170 g)

Transvaal Thick-tailed Scorpion ▲
Parabuthus transvaalicus
(up to 14 cm)

The tail and pincer size of a **scorpion** can indicate if the animal is venomous or not. The **Thick-tailed Scorpion** has a thick tail, slender pincers, and is dangerous to humans. It stings its prey, affecting the nervous system which causes paralysis or death to smaller creatures. The **Shiny Burrowing Scorpion** has a slender tail and large pincers, which give a painful but not deadly sting. Both Scorpions are active at night. During the day, the dangerous Thick-tailed species hides under stones, rocks or dead logs, while the Shiny Burrowing Scorpion burrows into the ground up to 1 metre deep.

▲ Shiny Burrowing Scorpion
Opistophthalmus glabrifrons
(5 - 12 cm)

▼ Sunspider (Solifuge)
Family Solifugidae **(2 - 5 cm)**
This nocturnal, spider-like creature is non-venomous, does not produce silk, and belongs to a group called the Solifuges. It can be identified by its large, formidable jaws used for killing prey, and the leg-like appendages in front (pedipalps), which give it the appearance of having ten legs.

◄ Common Cricket
Gryllus bimaculatus **(2,8 cm)**
These very noisy nocturnal insects will be heard around camp at night, when they emerge from hiding to feed. The chirping is made by males rubbing their forewings together to attract the females.

Scrub Hare ▼
Lepus saxatilis (L: 55 cm; 2 kg)
Scrub Hares live in open savannah with good grass cover. They are often spotted darting ahead of car lights at night. They eat grass, and will even eat their own pellets to extract all nutrients. They do not dig burrows but use dense grass cover for shelter.

◄ Pangolin
Manis temminckii
(L: 1,1 m; 7 - 10 kg)
The pangolin forages alone for termites and ants, using its large front claws to tear open termite mounds. It is covered in an armour of heavy scales and, in the same way as a hedgehog, rolls itself up into a protective ball to defend itself.

▼ Aardvark (Antbear)
Orycteropus afer (L: 1,4 - 1,8 m; 40 - 70 kg)
The aardvark is hardly ever seen by humans but plays a significant role in the wild (pages 20, 29, 37). It uses its strong, bear-like claws and 30-cm-long, sticky tongue to prey on ants and termites. The excavated termite mounds later become burrows for many animals such as hyaena, warthog, and even bats, owls and monitors. The aardvark has very poor eyesight, but uses its keen senses of smell and hearing to locate food.

◄ Peter's Epauletted Fruit-bat
Epomophorus crypturus
(L: 14 cm; 80 - 140 g)

These bats both roost during the day, in **colonies of a hundred or more.** They can be seen **flying around at dusk.** The **Little Free-tailed Bat** uses echolocation for navigation and to hunt flying insects, and it roosts in caves, roofs of houses and old mines. **Peter's Epauletted Fruit-bat** uses eyesight and smell to find its diet of ripe fruit, and spends the day in the dense foliage of trees.

Little Free-tailed Bat ▲
Tadarida pumila
(L: 9 cm; 11,5g)

Porcupine ►
Hystrix africaeaustralis
(L: 0,7 - 1 m; 10 - 24 kg)
The porcupine is Africa's largest rodent. It travels up to 20 km at night, foraging for bark, roots, bulbs and wild fruit. The impressive spines are hollow modified hairs which the porcupine raises and vibrates to ward off predators. Lion and leopard can be fatally injured if quills lodge in their paws or face, making hunting or feeding impossible.

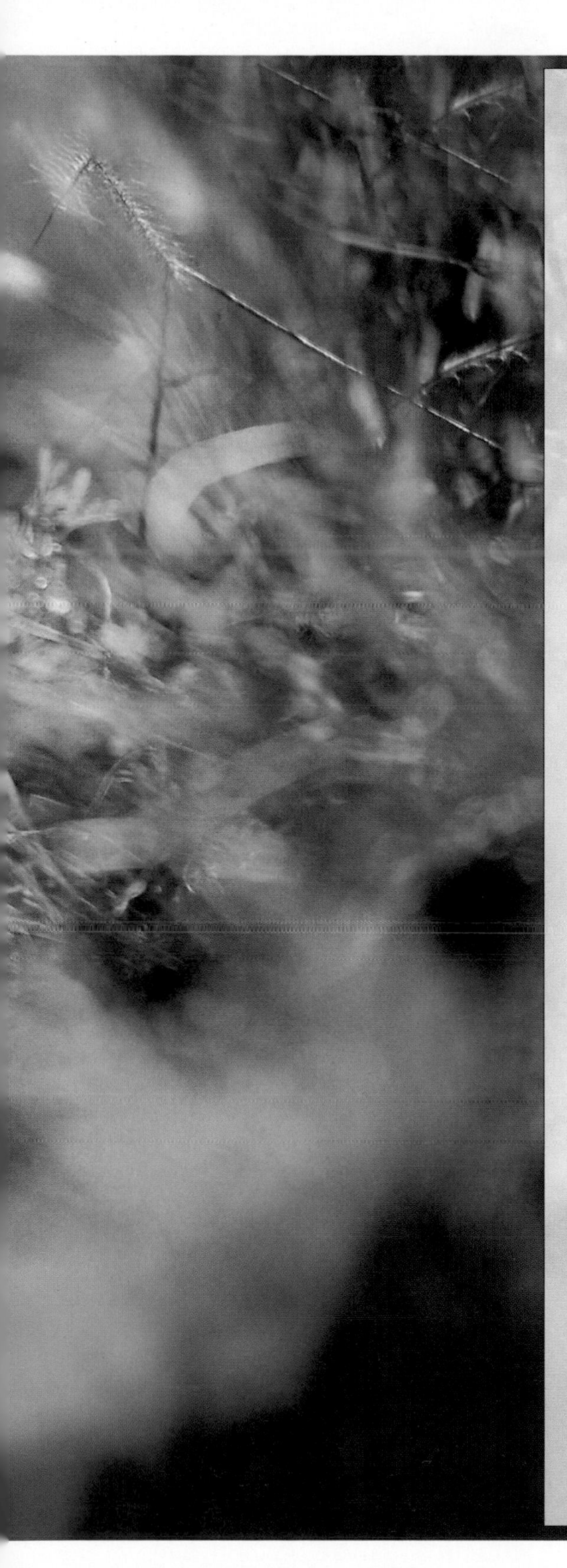

Reptiles, Amphibians and Fish

There is a greater diversity of reptiles than of mammals in southern Africa. They successfully inhabit most environments – on land and in water. These creatures are often overlooked in the search for the large and impressive mammals. However, reptiles, amphibians and fish have their own exciting equivalents of meat-eaters, grazers and browsers. Watching a lion kill large prey like a buffalo is thrilling, but a python catching a dove or antelope could be just as interesting, and is much more unusual to see.

Only a very few of the common and more obvious creatures are covered on these pages. They are intended merely as an introduction to a new and different world.

Reptiles and amphibians are not always considered the most likeable creatures, but their curious habits and adaptations to the environments they occupy, tell a fascinating story.

Reptiles, amphibians and fish are measured in length from tip of nose to tip of tail.

Before mating the male Leopard Tortoise 'bumps' the female into submission!

BRUCE LITTLE

Landbased Reptiles

Landbased reptiles have dry, scaly skin to protect them from the elements. They are all cold-blooded, needing the sun to keep them warm, but they differ enormously in appearance, habits and habitat.

Some species are strongly associated with specific trees, such as the Southern Tree Agama with Acacias. Tortoises and lizards use termitaria for breeding and often for hunting, while hollow tree trunks are favourite shelters for a wide variety of lizards, monitors and even the Southern African Python.

Monitors and pythons have been endangered by the fashion industry because of their attractive skins, but are now protected species. Monitors are most often sighted when disturbed, as they scuffle rapidly across the ground, vanishing to safety.

◄ **Leopard Tortoise**
Geochelone pardalis
(30 - 60 cm)

These two **tortoises** are widely distributed in South Africa. They are most active during or just after the rains, and hibernate during cold winter months. The **Leopard Tortoise** and the **Speke's Hinged Tortoise** eat plants and fruit, but the latter also preys on millipedes, beetles and snails. The hatchlings of both species are vulnerable to predation by carnivorous animals and birds. Hinged Tortoises are named after the unique hinge found at the back of the shell (of adults), which can be closed for protection.

Speke's Hinged Tortoise ▼
Kinixys spekei
(17 - 22 cm)

◄ **Praying Mantis**
Sphodromantis gastrica
(8 cm)

A slow-moving, predatory insect, it sits back on its hind legs holding its front legs out together as if praying. As soon as an insect passes by, the front legs shoot out and seize the prey. It is included here as it is a favourite prey of chameleons (below).

These three **lizard-like creatures** live above the ground. The **Tree Agama** gives a painful bite if teased by humans. It is often sighted on a tree trunk, where the blue head of a breeding male is unmistakeable. It may move to the ground to eat ants and termites. The **House Gecko** lives under tree bark, but may be seen actively hunting insects on the walls and roofs of homes at night. The males vigorously defend their territories, chasing or fighting off other males. A **Flap-neck Chameleon** can change colour to match its surroundings, thus escaping predators. It detects insects with its independently rotating eyes, and catches them with its 20-cm-long, sticky tongue. Rich folklore causes it to be feared by many tribes.

▼ **Flap-neck Chameleon**
Chamaeleo dilepis
(20 - 24 cm)

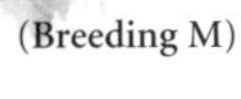
(Breeding M)

Southern Tree Agama ▲
Acanthocerus atricollis
(20 - 30 cm)

◄ **Moreau's Tropical House Gecko**
Hemidactylus mabouia
(12 - 16 cm)

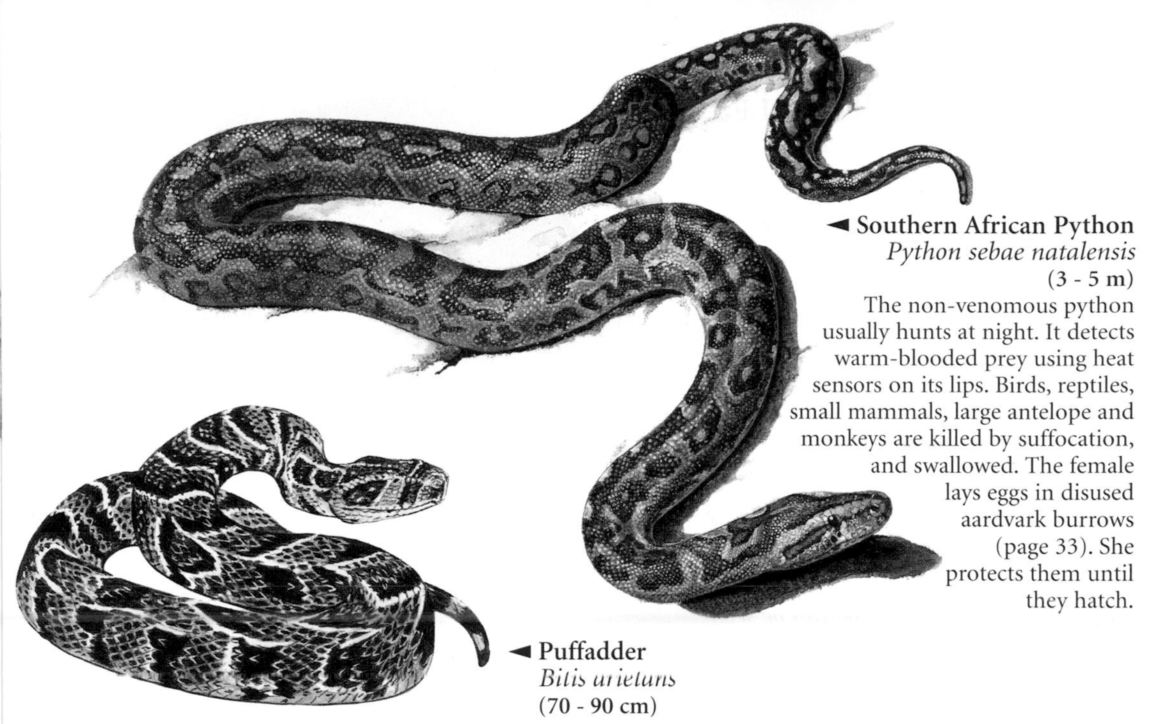

◄ **Southern African Python**
Python sebae natalensis
(3 - 5 m)
The non-venomous python usually hunts at night. It detects warm-blooded prey using heat sensors on its lips. Birds, reptiles, small mammals, large antelope and monkeys are killed by suffocation, and swallowed. The female lays eggs in disused aardvark burrows (page 33). She protects them until they hatch.

◄ **Puffadder**
Bitis arietans
(70 - 90 cm)

A bite from one of these **highly venomous** snakes can result in a human death. The **Puffadder** has a flattened, triangular head and moves with a sluggish, caterpillar-like motion. It lies in cover, waiting to ambush its prey. It will warn an intruder of its presence by uttering a deep hiss. The **Boomslang** is recognised by its blunt head and very large eyes. The colouration is variable: juveniles are twig-coloured, females are olive to brown, and males have various colour phases (one being illustrated here). It inflates its throat and will bite readily if threatened. It hunts during the day, and when it has caught the prey, will chew it, to inject the venom.

(M)

▲ **Boomslang**
Dispholidus typus
(1,2 - 1,5 m)

Rock Monitor ►
Varanus exanthematicus albigularis
(0,7 - 1,3 m)
This huge lizard eats tortoises, eggs, beetles, millipedes, small birds, rodents and carrion. It digs tunnels under rock overhangs, or uses old burrows or termite mounds to shelter, hibernate in winter or lay its eggs. The eggs can also be laid in soft, moist soil and are often eaten by the Banded Mongoose (page 30).

Giant Plated Lizard ▲
Gerrhosaurus validus **(40 - 60 cm)**
These lizards are omnivorous, eating plant material, insects, snails, millipedes and other lizards. They inhabit the upper area of large granite outcrops or koppies. They use the rocks for shelter, protection and breeding.

BIRDS

An interest in birds ensures that a trip into the Lowveld will always be rewarding.

Birds use a wide variety of habitats and food niches. The bills or beaks of birds tell a lot about their diet, and therefore about the food niche they occupy. Seed-eaters have small conical bills, and forage close to, or on, the ground; nectar-feeders have long thin bills, and feed on flowering trees or plants; many insect-eaters have hooked bills, and perch on a branch, waiting for prey to move within striking distance.

The larger predatory birds (raptors) often perch high in tall trees, where they scan the ground for prey. Otherwise they are sighted soaring and gliding above, searching for prey. Many raptors breed in winter, when the animals they eat are very active and easy to spot. In most predatory bird species, the females are larger than the males and therefore tend to catch prey.

Birds in South Africa are given a number recorded by the book, Roberts Birds of SA. Their numbers are used in this book. Sizes given are from beak-tip to tail-tip.

Cape Glossy Starlings are one of the most beautiful and common birds in the Lowveld.

BRUCE LITTLE

Drier Areas

Away from Water

This habitat is fairly dry, and has a greater number of species during summer. It includes the denser bush away from water, as well as the more open areas with fewer trees, such as the brackish sites. Different birds are found in different niches in drier bush. These have been divided into On or Near the Ground, Using Prominent Perches, and In the Canopy of Trees.

◄ **Crested Barbet**
Trachyphonus vaillantii **(23 cm) 473**
This barbet is unmistakeable with its thick bill and colourful plumage. It is highly vocal, the call sounding like a muffled alarm clock. The bill is used to dig nesting holes in tree trunks, where a pair raise up to four broods a year.

On or Near the Ground

These birds spend a lot of time looking for food on the ground. When flushed or threatened they may settle in bushes and trees. Many of them are conspicuous, and are easily spotted foraging. Their characteristic calls can be heard ringing through the savannah. Some bird calls are distinctive, attractive and easy to learn. These can help with bird identification, and will give you a new level of pleasure and awareness.

African Hoopoe ►
Upupa africana
(27 cm) 451
The African Hoopoe eats mainly caterpillars and worms, which it finds in the ground by probing with its long beak. It often erects its fan-shaped crest after landing, and flies as if its wings can't support its body weight. Its name is derived from its '*hoop-hoop*' call.

◄ **Arrow-marked Babbler**
Turdoides jardineii **(24 cm) 560**
Babblers move through the lower branches, from tree to tree, in a loose, noisy, babbling group of about ten birds. The group helps to build the nest in dense bush or trees, where only the dominant female breeds.

▲ **Emerald-spotted Wood-Dove (Greenspotted Dove)**
Turtur chalcospilos **(20 cm) 358**
Usually solitary or in pairs, the Emerald-spotted Wood-Dove is most often seen on sandy roads or on bare ground where it eats seeds, berries and termites. It has an unmistakable, melancholic call: *'Oh dear, dear, dear, dear'*.

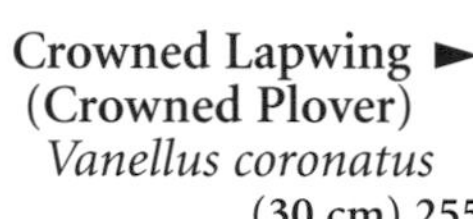

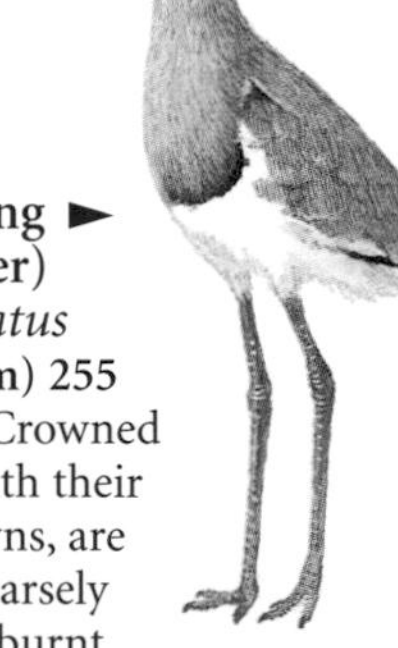

Crowned Lapwing ►
(Crowned Plover)
Vanellus coronatus
(30 cm) 255
Gregarious Crowned Lapwings, with their obvious crowns, are found in sparsely covered and burnt areas. They are renowned for their habit of dive-bombing intruders near their nests, with noisy screams.

Senegal Lapwing ►
(Lesser Black-wing Plover)
Vanellus lugubris **(24 cm) 256**
This migrant lapwing, with yellow-orange eyes and brown legs, is essentially a Mozambiquan bird, but can sometimes be seen here at the western point of its range. It favours dry savannah, and especially burnt or heavily grazed areas. It is nomadic, occurring in small parties.

◄ **Common Ostrich**
Struthio camelus (**H: 2 m; 156 kg; speed: 70 km/h) 1**
This species is the largest living bird on Earth. The male ostrich shown here, can easily be identified by its black feather plumes. His shins turn red during the breeding season. Paler feathered females are often seen performing a 'broken wing' act, when a vehicle passes a group of young chicks.

(M)

Red-billed Buffalo-Weaver ►
Bubalornis niger
(21 cm) 798
The nest of this weaver is a large and conspicuous, untidy mass of thorny twigs and sticks, high up in the branches of a tree. The weavers breed communally, and each pair has its own entrance and tunnel into a nest.

◄ **Southern Ground-Hornbill**
Bucorvus leadbeateri
(1,1 m) 463

(M)

◄ **Red-crested Korhaan**
Eupodotis ruficrista
(50 cm) 237

These **four larger ground birds** spend most of their time on the ground, and are only seen flying when threatened or displaying. The **Red-crested Korhaan** is the only species in this group that doesn't roost in trees at night. When threatened it stands still, using camouflage to hide in the bush. The male displays a red crest when courting. It makes distinctive tongue-clicking sounds, then loud, short, piping calls, and often a spectacular, directly upward flight with a 'plummet' back to the ground. The **Southern Ground-Hornbills** look like large turkeys, and have a deep, booming call, often heard at dawn. The birds stalk through the veld in pairs or groups looking for snails, frogs, insects, small mammals and reptiles. **Crested Francolins** scratch and peck the ground in pairs or small groups for seeds, berries and grubs. Their repeated call – a loud, crowing *'chak, kikwerri-kwetchi'* – is characteristic of the Lowveld at dawn and dusk. **Guineafowl,** which gather in flocks, are among our best-loved and noisiest birds, their call also being characteristic of rural Africa.

◄ **Helmeted Guineafowl**
Numida meleagris
(53 - 58 cm) 203

▲ **Crested Francolin**
Peliperdix sephaena
(32 cm) 189

Drier Areas

On or Near the Ground

Although these birds are often seen foraging on the ground, many are first spotted in bushes or trees where they escape danger and build their nests. A number of them are a common sight around human habitation. Here, they benefit from the shorter grass that exposes seeds and insects, and makes food easier to find.

(M)

▲ **Golden-breasted Bunting**
Emberiza flaviventris (16 cm) 884
The Golden-breasted Bunting is most often seen walking on the ground beneath bushes or trees, foraging for insects and seeds. It is easily recognised by its golden breast and black-and-white striped head. The nest is a cup of grass stems and roots, normally in the fork of a small tree.

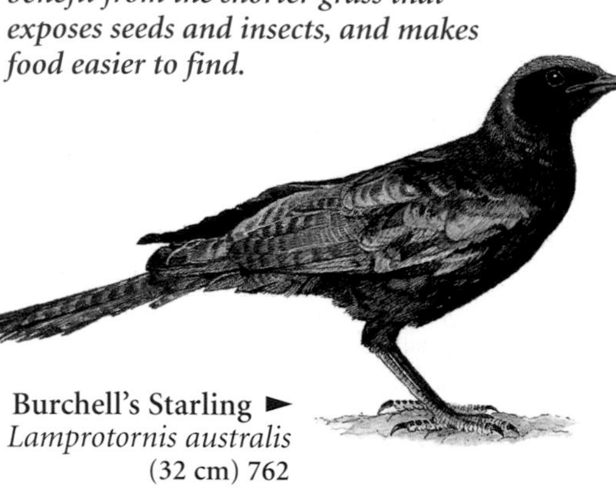

Burchell's Starling ►
Lamprotornis australis
(32 cm) 762

◄ **Cape Glossy Starling**
Lamprotornis nitens
(22 cm) 764

Starlings are **gregarious and the different species intermingle**, often becoming very tame around camp. In bright sunlight, they glisten a dark, metallic green, but on a dull, overcast day you will see the splendid subtleties of colour. **Burchell's Starlings** are normally found where trees are taller and denser. **Cape Glossy Starlings** can be a delight, performing aerobatics before roosting at night. They often perch in treetops, calling with a loud, harsh, high-pitched croaking.

Cape Turtle-Dove ▲
Streptopelia capicola
(28 cm) 354

Both these **doves forage for seeds and insects** on the ground. The **Cape Turtle-Dove** has a thin, black collar round the back of the neck. Males display by flapping straight upward, and then coo-ing while spiralling back down to their perch. Most easily recognised by its pinky, spotted chest, the **Laughing Dove** is a common resident. Males pursue females along a branch or on the ground, with a comic hunched, hopping gait.

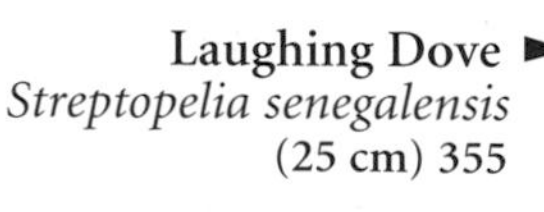

Laughing Dove ►
Streptopelia senegalensis
(25 cm) 355

◄ **White-browed Scrub-Robin (White-breasted Robin)**
Cercotrichas leucophrys
(15 cm) 613
Usually solitary, this robin often hides in tangled scrub. It hops while foraging for insects and spiders, and may flick its tail up and down, especially if alarmed.

◄ **Red-billed Hornbill**
Tockus erythrorhynchus
(46 cm) 458

The **nesting behaviour of both these hornbills is similar**. The females are sealed in a hole in a tree, so that only the beak protrudes. The male feeds the female during this period. After the first egg hatches she breaks out, and the nestlings reseal the opening. Both the **Red-billed** and **Southern Yellow-billed Hornbills'** calls are a very similar '*wak wak wak*' which speeds up into double notes of a duet '*kawak kawak kawak*' and sounds like '*go back go back go back*'.

◄ **Southern Yellow-billed Hornbill**
Tockus leucomelas
(48 - 60 cm) 459

Blue Waxbill ►
Uraeginthus angolensis
(13 cm) 844
(M)

These three small birds are **often found in bird parties** and they can become tame around human habitation. They may be seen feeding on the ground in pairs (when breeding) or in small groups. The **Blue Waxbill** is recognised by its delicate blue face and breast. It feeds in small flocks (up to 40), and flies rapidly into dense bush if alarmed. The bright yellow rump and white-tipped tail of the **Yellow-fronted Canary**, identifies it in flight. The males sing a whistling chirp (sometimes together) from a conspicuous perch. The **Red-billed Firefinch** is a remarkable red, with a pink bill. Like the Blue Waxbill, it flies to the nearest cover when disturbed.

Yellow-fronted Canary ►
Serinus mozambicus
(12 cm) 869

Red-billed Firefinch ►
Lagonosticta senegala
(10 cm) 842
(M) *(F)*

Drier Bush

In the Canopy of Trees

The birds on this page are usually found within the canopy of bushes and trees. As with other animals, birds are specially adapted for a specific food niche. Some forage for fruit; some take insects from leaves and stems; while others search the bark and trunk for caterpillars. The woodpeckers have two toes facing forward and two backward, to provide a good grip on the tree. The hard skull is cushioned by muscles to absorb the impact of continual pecking.

Many birds associate in groups or flocks. This behaviour helps the birds to survive, through increased vigilance and protection.

◄ **Red-faced Mousebird**
Urocolius indicus
(34 cm) 426

The small Red-faced Mousebird looks a little like a parakeet. It has a crest and a parrot-shaped, fruit-eating beak. Flocks of 5 - 20 birds can be seen creeping and crawling through the vegetation like mice.

▲ **Brown-headed Parrot**
Poicephalus cryptoxanthus
(23 cm) 363

Brown-headed Parrots are often seen in small groups, screeching with typical parrot-like whistles. They clamber about in flowering or fruiting trees, eating fruit, nuts, nectar and seeds. Up to 50 birds can be found together at a good food source.

◄ **Green Wood-Hoopoe (Red-billed Woodhoopoe)**
Phoeniculus purpureus
(34 cm) 452

Green Wood-Hoopoes are common, noisy birds found in groups of 2 - 16, with one breeding pair in the group. They may be seen examining tree trunks and branches for insects, millipedes and lizards. When calling, they rock back and forth cackling loudly, which is likened to laughing women in a number of vernacular names.

The two **small birds** below **eat insects**, and may join mixed bird parties. The **Southern Black Tit** enjoys caterpillars, which it finds under bark or in seedpods. They live in pairs or small groups, and prefer moister habitats. The **Chinspot Batis** can be heard calling constantly, *'weep woop'* or *'weep woop wurp'*, sounding like *'three blind mice'*. It often hangs upside down to remove its prey, frequently spiders, from leaves. It lives alone or in pairs, preferring drier bush.

Southern Black Tit ▲
Parus niger
(16 cm) 554

(F)

(M)

▲ **Chinspot Batis**
Batis molitor
(13 cm) 701

Woodpeckers **scurry around dead trees, knocking the wood with their beaks** to open up caterpillar tunnels. The sound of tapping on dry wood carries for long distances. The birds usually land low on the tree and work their way upwards. The **Golden-tailed Woodpecker** can be distinguished by the heavy streaking on its cheeks and throat, and the **Cardinal Woodpecker** by its brown forehead.

◄ **Golden-tailed Woodpecker**
Campethera abingoni
(20 cm) 483

Cardinal Woodpecker ►
Dendropicos fuscescens
(15 cm) 486

(M)

Marico Sunbird ►
Cinnyris mariquensis
(14 cm) 779

The female of the Marico Sunbird lacks the bright colours of the male, but she has her own delicate beauty. They are found alone or in pairs in Acacia savannah. They use their long, curved beaks to probe nectar from flowers, and to catch insects in the air.

◄ **Woodland Kingfisher**
Halcyon senegalensis
(22 - 24 cm) 433

These three species are all **common summer migrants** (October to April) from further north in Africa. The **Woodland Kingfisher** flashes bright, light blue, while perching, or flying low in tree canopies. It usually nests in old barbet or woodpecker holes, and eats insects, small reptiles and frogs, and, rarely, fish. Cuckoos lay their eggs in the nests of other birds, who then rear the nestlings. The **Diderick Cuckoo** may parasitise weaver and sparrow nests. With its distinctive *'dee-dee-deedereek'* call, it is more often heard than seen. The **Jacobin Cuckoo** parasitises mainly Fork-tailed Drongo and Dark-Capped Bulbul nests. The male distracts the host so that the female can lay her eggs.

◄ **Diderick Cuckoo**
Chrysococcyx caprius
(19 cm) 386

▲ **Jacobin Cuckoo**
Oxylophus jacobinus
(34 cm) 382

Dense Bush

Near Water

These birds live in the large trees and dense bush close to rivers. Many of them are also found around camp gardens that have water. They forage in the canopies for fruit and insects, and are therefore difficult to find. Bright colouration, sudden movement or bird calls give them away.

In these moist habitats, there is often a great concentration of birds around flowering and fruiting trees. Many of them enjoy figs and other fruit. They help with germination by partly digesting and softening the seed capsules. Birds that eat flowers and nectar play a vital role in cross-pollination as the pollen sticks to their beaks. The birds are therefore invaluable in the life-cycle of some of the riverine trees.

Walk quietly around camp with a pair of binoculars. You might be able to see a number of birds that you have only been able to hear in the bushes while driving around.

◄ **Trumpeter Hornbill**
Bycanistes bucinator
(62 cm) 455

Crowned Hornbill ►
Tockus alboterminatus
(50 cm) 460

Both the hornbills and the African Green-Pigeon are **gregarious and eat fruit**, especially figs. They are often found eating together in fig trees (page 11). The hornbills are fascinating birds with a conspicuous, horny ridge (casque) on top of their bills. In the **Trumpeter Hornbill**, the casque is hollow, and may be used to amplify the long, trumpet-like calls that sound like a baby crying. The **Crowned Hornbill** is smaller and often seen in flocks flying above rivers, calling shrilly, '*pi-pi-pi-pi*'. The **African Green-Pigeon** hangs upside down like a parrot to reach ripe fruit. Its green plumage provides excellent camouflage within the leafy canopy. While Green-Pigeons only eat fruit, Trumpeter Hornbills also eat large insects.

Black-collared Barbet ►
Lybius torquatus
(20 cm) 464
A highly vocal bird (especially in summer during breeding), the Black-collared Barbet is recognised by its red head and black collar. Its call is a quickly repeated duet. The male calls '*hoop*' first, immediately followed by the '*pud-duh-ly*' of the female. It eats fruit (especially figs) and insects.

▲**African Green-Pigeon**
Treron calva
(30 cm) 361

▼ Purple-crested Turaco (Purple-crested Lourie)
Musophaga porphyreolophus
(42 cm) 371
These striking birds hide in the canopy, running agilely along the branches, foraging for fruit and buds. Their conspicuous crimson wings may be spotted as they glide through thick canopies. They call repeatedly and together *'kok-kok-kok'*, which rises in volume and excitement.

Dark-capped Bulbul ► (Black-eyed Bulbul)
Pycnonotus tricolor
(22 cm) 568
A lively, liquid call is characteristic and uttered while foraging for fruit and insects. They are very noisy, territorial birds, and will quickly sound their alarm call, *'chissik chissik'*, when a snake, owl or mongoose is near.

White-bellied Sunbird ►
Cinnyris talatala
(11 cm) 787
on Plumbago (page 12)

(M)

Both these sunbirds are **often seen around lodges or camps** with flowering trees. They eat nectar, which is sucked up with a tube-like tongue, and insects. Nests are made of grass, leaves and other material, bound with spider's web and suspended from a branch of a tree or bush. Although female sunbirds appear drab, the males are spectacular. The male **white-bellied Sunbird** has a unique metallic-green head and throat, with a white belly; the male **Scarlet-chested Sunbird** has a large, diagnostic scarlet chest patch.

◄ Black-headed Oriole
Oriolus larvatus
(25 cm) 545
This enchanting bird moves in the tops of tall trees, calling in beautiful liquid notes. It eats insects, berries and nectar. The nest hangs hammock-like from a slender branch, and is made of stringy lichen, moss and grass, bound with spider's web.

▲ Scarlet-chested Sunbird
Chalcomitra senegalensis
(14 cm) 791
on Weeping Boer-bean (page 10)

Dense Bush

Near Water (continued)

All these birds eat insects and other small animals. Some of them forage on the ground, while others move through the canopy of trees searching for prey. Except for the ground-nesting Natal Francolin, they all build their nests within the tree canopies. The nests are either well-camouflaged, or inaccessible to predators. They are not, however, completely out of danger. Snakes can wind their way up trees and into weaver nests even though they appear well protected.

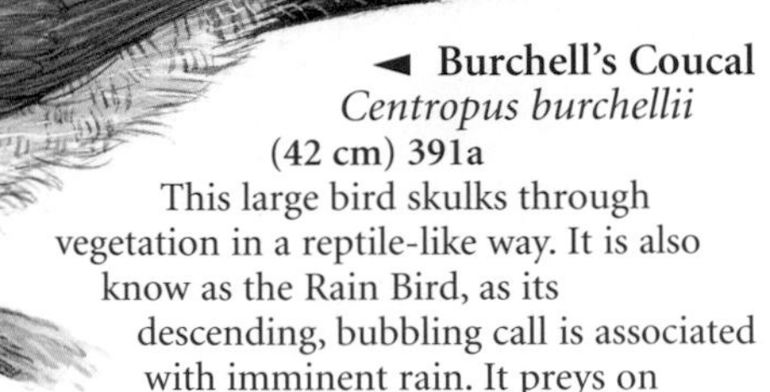

◄ **Burchell's Coucal**
Centropus burchellii
(42 cm) 391a
This large bird skulks through vegetation in a reptile-like way. It is also know as the Rain Bird, as its descending, bubbling call is associated with imminent rain. It preys on insects, small frogs, reptiles, nestling birds, and mammals.

African Paradise-Flycatcher ►
Terpsiphone viridis
(23 cm, tail 18 cm [M], 17 cm [F]) 710
Common in rest camps, the Paradise-Flycatcher catches small insects on the wing. The male has incredibly long tail feathers that trail out behind him as he flies. Paradise-Flycatchers have a tiny nest bound with spider's web and camouflaged with plant fibres and lichen, usually in the fork of a tree.

(M)

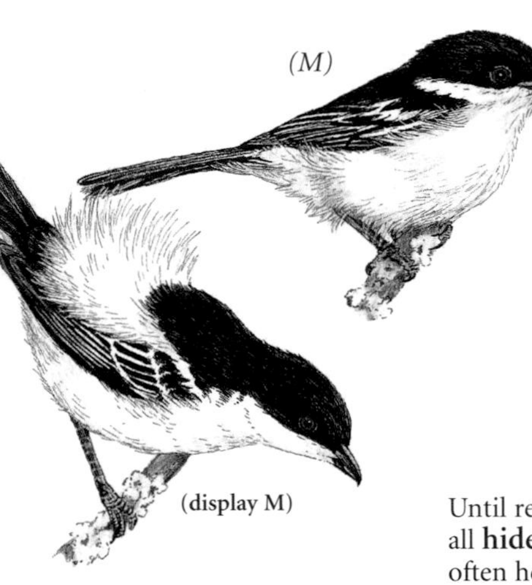

(M)

(display M)

▲ **Black-backed Puffback (Puffback)**
Dryoscopus cubla
(18 cm) 740

Until recently all three of these birds **were called 'shrikes'**. They all **hide and crawl through dense vegetation** and are more often heard than seen, each with its own very distinctive call. The **Black-backed Puffback** also forages high in the trees, seldom venturing lower down. It calls '*chick, weeo*' in loud, repetitive, click-whistling notes. During courtship, the male puffs up his splendid, gleaming white back or rump feathers. The beautiful **Orange-breasted Bush-Shrike** tends to move in the tops of trees. Its call is like Morse code, in 5 - 8 '*poo-poo-poo-poooo*' notes. The shy **Southern Boubou** keeps to thick undergrowth and lower branches. The males and females call constantly to each other to keep in touch. The duet is variable, with a basic '*boo-boo*' followed by a whistled '*whee-ooo*'.

Orange-breasted Bush-Shrike ►
Telophorus sulfureopectus
(18 - 19 cm) 748

(M)

(M)

Southern Boubou ►
Laniarius ferrugineus
(21 - 23 cm) 736

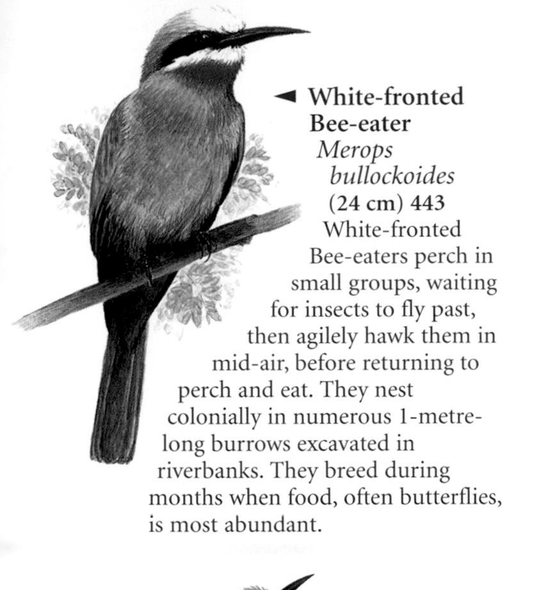

◄ **White-fronted Bee-eater**
Merops bullockoides
(24 cm) 443
White-fronted Bee-eaters perch in small groups, waiting for insects to fly past, then agilely hawk them in mid-air, before returning to perch and eat. They nest colonially in numerous 1-metre-long burrows excavated in riverbanks. They breed during months when food, often butterflies, is most abundant.

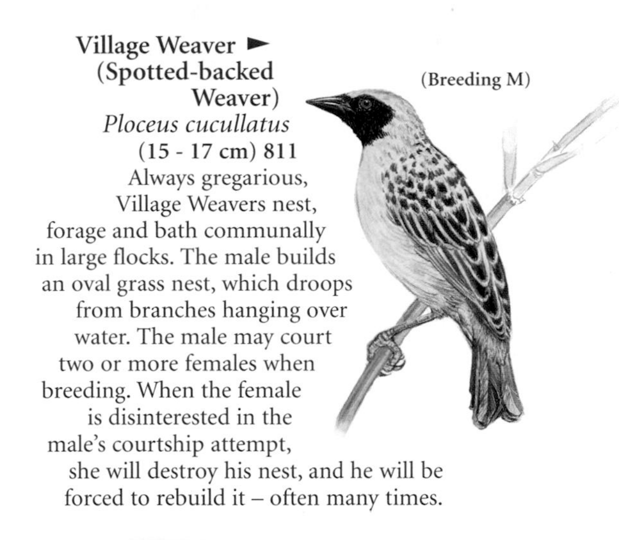

(Breeding M)

Village Weaver ► (Spotted-backed Weaver)
Ploceus cucullatus
(15 - 17 cm) 811
Always gregarious, Village Weavers nest, forage and bath communally in large flocks. The male builds an oval grass nest, which droops from branches hanging over water. The male may court two or more females when breeding. When the female is disinterested in the male's courtship attempt, she will destroy his nest, and he will be forced to rebuild it – often many times.

Little Bee-eater ▲
Merops pusillus
(17 cm) 444
This beautiful, little bird is fairly common in the Lowveld and breeds in summer. It is often seen hawking insects from a branch.

Natal Francolin ►
Pternistes natalensis
(36 cm) 196

These three birds are **ground foragers in moister areas. Natal Francolins** can be heard calling at dawn and dusk in a repeated raucous, crowing *'kwadi kwadi kwadi'*. They move in pairs or parties of up to ten, eating snails, insects, roots, fruit and seeds. The **Hadeda Ibis**' call is also a well-loved sound in South Africa. They call '*Ha ha ... Hadeda*' when disturbed, or when leaving their roosts in the morning. They probe into the ground with their long, curved bills, or peck up insects, snails, reptiles and earthworms. The **Kurrichane Thrush** is usually alone, or in pairs, running in short bursts, and then stopping to peck the ground for insects and lizards.

◄ **Hadeda Ibis**
Bostrychia hagedash
(76 cm) 94

Kurrichane Thrush ►
Turdus libonyanus
(22 cm) 576

Open Water

Waterbirds are specifically associated with open water habitats, such as rivers, pans, lakes and dams. As in other habitats, the birds use different niches to eat and breed. Some birds wade in the shallow water, while others swim and dive where it is deeper. Lapwings prefer the open ground surrounding the water, and Crakes and Jacanas are agile on floating water plants. Kingfishers prefer higher vantage points to scan the water for prey.

The open water habitat is one of the easiest places to spot and identify birds, because many are conspicuous and exposed.

◄ Dragonfly
Anisoptera species
(4,5 - 14 cm)
Found at the edges of ponds and streams, the males defend their territories by attacking or chasing away intruders. The male and female may be seen flying together in tandem as they mate, occasionally flicking over the water so the female can lay her eggs on the surface. Eggs then drift gently to the bottom and hatch a few days later.

Damselfly ►
Zygoptera species
(15 - 50 mm)
The damselfly folds its wings together when resting - the dragonfly holds its wings out horizontally. Like the dragonfly, the damselfly preys on insects, and lays its eggs in water. The adults can be found far from water, where they escape predation and search for prey.

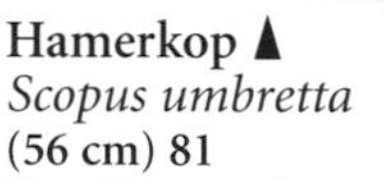

Hamerkop ▲
Scopus umbretta
(56 cm) 81
Usually seen alone or in pairs, the Hamerkop has a conspicuous hammer-shaped head. It may either patrol the shallows for frogs and tadpoles, or snatch morsels from the water surface in flight. A breeding pair use sticks and reeds to build a huge, dome-shaped nest (up to 2 metres in diameter) in the forks of large trees, near water.

▲ Yellow-billed Duck
Anas undulata **(51 - 63) 104**
They are found in pairs, and may be seen feeding on plant matter, bottoms-up, on dams and perennial rivers. Their yellow bills are conspicuous and make identification easy.

Blacksmith Lapwing ►
(Blacksmith Plover)
Vanellus armatus **(30 cm) 258**
Found in pairs or small groups, Blacksmith Lapwings eat and nest on the shorelines of water. They are extremely vocal and aggressive, 'screeching' and dive-bombing predators when their nest is threatened. The nest is simply an exposed scrape in the soil, but the eggs are well camouflaged.

Giant Kingfisher ►
Megaceryle maxima
(46 cm) 429

▲ **Pied Kingfisher** ►
Ceryle rudis
(25 - 29 cm) 428

Both these **kingfishers eat fish**, their favourite branches often being coated in fish scales. **Pied Kingfishers** hover above water with miraculously fast wingbeats, then plunge in head-first, returning to a perch to kill their catch. They also eat shellfish and insects. **Giant Kingfishers** perch over water, looking for fish, crabs or frogs within range. Both these species nest in tunnels burrowed into river or stream banks.

African Pied Wagtail ►
Motacilla aguimp
(20 cm) 711
The black-and-white Pied Wagtail may be seen walking around on rocks or sandbanks. It suddenly chases or leaps after crawling or flying insects, such as dragonflies. It regularly bobs its tail up and down, especially on landing or when agitated. It becomes tame around human habitation.

▼ **Little Grebe (Dabchick)**
Tachybaptus ruficollis
(20 cm) 8
These handsome little birds are common on all the dams in the the Lowveld. The easiest way to identify them – apart from their reddish face and 'tail in the air' posture – is by the way they continuously dive under water. Their nests are floating plattforms made of weeds.

▼ **Black Crake**
Amaurornis flavirostra (21 cm) 213
The bright red legs and eyes, and yellow beak of the Black Crake, are a striking contrast to the black body. It is usually seen walking over floating vegetation in reedy or marshy areas. Its high-pitched clucking, and deep growling bullfrog-like calls can be heard in reedbeds. It eats insects, snails, crabs, worms, small fish, small birds, herons' eggs, seeds and water plants.

African Jacana ▲
Actophilornis africanus (28 cm) 240
Also known as lily-trotters, African Jacanas walk on floating plants to move about the water surface hunting for insects, crustaceans and snails. They have exceptionally long toes, for balance and to spread their weight. The male looks after the eggs and chicks, carrying them around under his wings, while the female finds her next mate of the season.

Open Water (continued)

Waterbirds are all well adapted to their environment. The large wading birds have long legs, giving them a good view of any prey swimming beneath the water surface. Fish-eating birds swallow fish head-first so that the scales and spines are folded flat. Saddle-billed Storks may snip the spines off larger fish before swallowing. Darters, herons and cormorants are often found nesting communally in trees, giving them safety in numbers.

◄ **African Fish-Eagle**
Haliaeetus vocifer
(63 - 73 cm) **148**
This exceptional eagle is usually first noticed as a white patch high in a tree overlooking an expanse of water. It has a magnificent ringing call, given while perching, or circling high overhead. It snatches fish near the water surface with its talons, eating larger ones on the ground, next to the water.

Common Moorhen ▼
Gallinula chloropus
(30 - 60 cm) **226**
A shy bird, it can be spotted swimming between vegetated patches in dams and river pools. It is an omnivore found alone or in small family groups.

◄ **White-breasted Cormorant**
Phalacrocorax lucidus
(90 cm) 55

These two birds **dive for fish and frogs.**
Cormorants cement their nest together with their guano. They often use the same nest of sticks year after year. **Darters** were known as 'snake birds' because their kinked necks appear snake-like when they swim. They spear their prey with dagger-like beaks. Their feathers absorb more water than other waterbirds. This makes them less buoyant, and enables them to dive deeper into the water, than other birds, in pursuit of their prey. After swimming, they are often seen standing on rocks or stumps, holding their wings out to dry.

◄ **Egyptian Goose**
Alopochen aegyptiacus
(70 cm) 102
Very widespread, Egyptian Geese make a great deal of noise before take-off, and during flight. The female 'honks' rapidly, *'honk-haah-haah-haah-haah'*, while the male hisses. They eat aquatic plants, grass and seedlings. Pairs mate for life, but when not breeding they gather in large groups on sandbanks.

African Darter ►
Anhinga rufa
(79 cm) **60**

(Breeding M)

◄ **Saddle-billed Stork**
Ephippiorhynchus senegalensis
(1,4 m) 88
The Saddle-billed Stork is a huge, impressive, endangered bird with a bright yellow, red and black bill. The male has brown eyes, and yellow wattles below them. The female has yellow eyes, but no wattles. Seen on its own or in pairs, this shy bird either walks slowly through shallow water looking for prey, or stands and waits for large fish, frogs and crabs to swim within range.

(M)

◄ **White-faced Duck**
Dendrocygna viduata
(48 cm) 99
A beautifully marked bird, the White-faced Duck has a very upright stance. It may be seen in huge numbers around the edges of water, or heard flying in whistling flocks.

▼ **Grey Heron**
Ardea cinerea
(1 m) 62

Goliath Heron ▼
Ardea goliath
(1,4 m) 64

Both **solitary birds**, these herons stand in shallow water for long periods, waiting for a passing fish, which they snap up with their long, sharp bills. They also eat frogs, insects, reptiles, small mammals and birds. They build a platform of sticks on trees or in reedbeds. The **Grey Heron** roosts and nests communally. The **Goliath Heron** usually nests alone, only occasionally with other herons.

Green-backed Heron ▼
Butorides striatus **(40 cm) 74**
This small, squat heron prefers denser vegetation. It is shy and solitary, and skulks around reeds and branches. It stands still for long periods, in a typical hunched posture, waiting for fish and frogs. It is unique in using bait such as live insects, as well as twigs, leaves and feathers, to lure fish within range of its dagger-like bill.

Nocturnal Birds

The night fliers – both birds and bats – use yet another part of the ecosystem and its habitats. Bats are on page 33.

Nocturnal birds use their sharp eyes and ears to spot prey, swooping down to land on the prey, or snatching it from the air. The night birds add a fascination, with very distinct, separate calls. Once these are known, the birds can be easily identified by visitors sitting around the campfire at night.

◄ **African Scops-Owl (Scops Owl)**
Otus senegalensis
(18 - 20 cm) 396
These tiny owls make an insect-like *'pirrp'* call. When disturbed by day, they elongate their bodies, lean sideways, extend their ear muffs, and almost close their eyes – and in doing so, resemble the branches on which they roost.

Marsh Owl ►
Asio capensis
(36 - 37 cm) 395
This ground-nesting owl is usually found in grassy areas of vleis and marshes. It hunts by flying low over grass, dropping suddenly onto prey such as rats and other rodents. The Marsh Owl's numbers are declining due to habitat loss.

Lunar Moths ▲
(Agema mimosae)
(wingspan: 120 mm)
are nocturnal, and their larvae feed on Marula (page 3) or Tamboti (page 11).

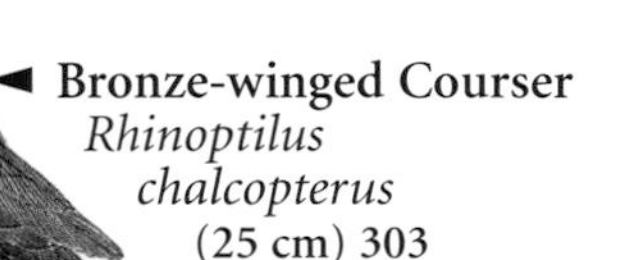

◄ **Bronze-winged Courser**
Rhinoptilus chalcopterus
(25 cm) 303

▼ **Spotted Thick-knee (Spotted Dikkop)**
Burhinus capensis
(44 cm) 297

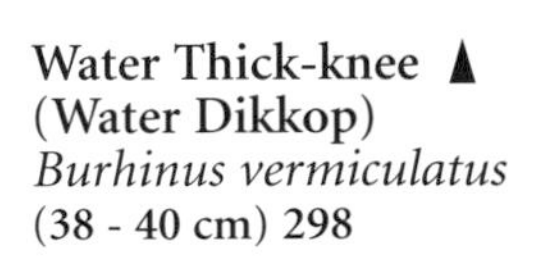

Water Thick-knee ▲
(Water Dikkop)
Burhinus vermiculatus
(38 - 40 cm) 298

These three **long-legged, ground-based** birds shelter in the bushes during the day, and appear at night to forage on insects. The Thick-knees also eat crustaceans and molluscs. The plover-like **Bronze-winged Courser**, with its red legs, is often spotted on the roads at night. They may freeze, or fly a short distance, to escape the intrusion. The **Water Thick-knee** lives near water, and is recognised by its conspicuous grey wing-bar. The **Spotted Thick-knee** is found in open savannah. When disturbed, Thick-knees run with their heads held low. The characteristic night-time calls are similar – a piping *'ti ti ti ti'* rising in pitch and volume, then dying down to a *'tee tee'*.

◄ **Cream-striped Owl Moth**
Cycligramma latona
(wingspan: 62 mm)
Very common, Cream-striped Owl Moths are attracted to artificial light, and may be seen resting on the walls of houses. They can hear the high-frequency sounds insectivorous bats emit when hunting them, and thus avoid being caught.

The **Eagle-owls** are the **largest owls in Africa**. The **Verreaux's Eagle-Owl** is the largest of all and can be identified by its pink eyelids. It makes a distinctive, grunt-like hooting call. Its diet consists of mammals as big as Vervet Monkeys (page 31), birds (including raptors), reptiles, frogs and fish. The **Spotted Eagle-Owl** has distinctive yellow eyes and conspicuous ear tufts, and calls a characterisitc hooting *'hu hoo'*. It eats mostly mice and insects, but also other animals.

▲ **Verreaux's Eagle-Owl (Giant Eagle-Owl)**
Bubo lacteus
(60 - 65 cm) 402

◄ **Spotted Eagle-Owl**
Bubo africanus
(47 cm) 401

Pearl-spotted Owlet ►
Glaucidium perlatum
(18 - 19 cm) 398
One of the smallest owls in southern Africa, the Pearl-spotted Owlet is often seen or heard in the day. It has a distinctive, long, repetitive, whistle-like call, ascending *'tiu tiu tiu tiu tiu'*, then descending, *'teeu teeu teeu'*. It hunts insects, rodents, reptiles, birds up to dove-size, and bats. It has two dark spots, or mock eyes, on the back of its head to confuse predators as to which way it is facing.

Fiery-necked Nightjar ▼
Caprimulgus pectoralis **(24 cm) 405**
The Fiery-necked Nightjar is often seen roosting or nesting on the ground. It is very well camouflaged, has long, pointed wings, and flies silently as it hawks insects from the air. It calls *'good lord'* in an initial rising whistle, ending in a series of falling trills *'deliver us'*.

Human History

The savannah country of the Lowveld and its nearby mountain ranges have a diverse human history. Over millennia, it has been home to a variety of people including the Stone Age San, farmers, metal-workers, early traders, gold-diggers and settlers from Europe.

The lush vegetation and plentiful wildlife of the subtropical Lowveld have supported a growing human population. However, searing heat and pests such as tsetse fly and mosquito brought quick death to many of those who ventured into the area.

Braving the Lowveld's unforgiving climate and wild exterior, many strong and determined people survived to exploit its significant riches. The legacy of their creative and inventive spirit is evident in both ancient and contemporary ruins and preserved sites scattered across the Lowveld.

In this section, the term BP refers to the number of years Before Present time.

Further reading:
- *The Kruger National Park – A Social and Political History by Jane Carruthers;*
- *A Beginner's Guide – Images of Power by David Lewis-Williams and Thomas Dowson;*
- *Field Guide to Rock Art – Fragile Heritage by David Lewis-Williams and Geoffrey Blundell.*

Spotting humans – from the bonnet of a 1940s Chevrolet – can be fun too!

STEVENSON-HAMILTON ARCHIVES

Early History

The early human history of the Lowveld has been overshadowed by its later history of European exploration and settlement. Archaeological work has, however, uncovered indisputable and fascinating evidence of indigenous communities thousands of years before the arrival of people from other lands and continents.

Stone and Iron Age peoples utilised the area, hunting, gathering and eventually planting crops, and forging iron. Theirs is a history integral to the Lowveld – as rich and varied as the area itself.

Fragments of red and yellow ochre, used by the San as pigments

San bow and poison-tipped arrow

San rock painting found in the Lowveld

The Stone Age

Bushveld Candelabra Euphorbia (*Euphorbia cooperi*) has highly toxic milky latex

One and a half million years ago, ancient humans (*Homo erectus*) inhabited the Lowveld, scavenging, foraging and hunting the prehistoric ancestors of the elephant, the giraffe and the baboon. By the Later Stone Age (beginning 40 000 BP), nomadic hunter-gatherers were living here. Known as the San people, they were modern humans (*Homo sapiens*) and skilful hunters, using a variety of weapons and implements made from bone, flint and animal skin. Hunting became easier once poison was used on arrow heads. The poison was extracted from the Poison Bush (*Acokanthera oppositifolia*), some Euphorbias, as well as the venom of snakes and spiders. It is now believed that these discoveries made it possible to hunt larger game, and gave humans more time to develop spiritually and culturally.

The San were artists and inventors, with strong spiritual beliefs and rituals that connected them intimately with the land and with the spirit world. Rock paintings depict this relationship. The rocks were painted with their fingers as well as feathers and brushes which the San made from animal hair.

A San hunter

Photo taken in 1800s of people working at an Iron Age smelting oven

Rock painting of San woman with a digging stick

The Iron Age

Evidence of the San's existence over thousands of years can be seen in the many engravings, rock paintings, tools and weapons that have been excavated and preserved at sites throughout the Lowveld. For centuries, they lived without competition from other humans, for resources. But from 1800 BP, African farmers began migrating to the area from central parts of the continent, bringing with them domestic animals and a knowledge of metal-work and crop-growing.

This marked the beginning of the Iron Age in southern Africa. The newcomers mined and worked metal such as iron and copper, and were able to extract gold from the surrounding rock to make ornaments. The mountain caves which were abundant in the area, provided shelter for Iron Age people although they also constructed dwellings. In one such cave outside Lydenburg, remains of clay masks, probably used for religious or initiation ceremonies and carbon-dated to 1500 BP, have been found.

Iron Age people also practised agriculture, planting crops such as sorghum and beans, and keeping sheep, cattle and goats. Their wattle and mud hut settlements were common along the banks of the Lowveld rivers. By the 15th Century, many African farmers had migrated to the area. This forced some of the San to retreat further south while others were incorporated into the 'new' economy and society.

Presence of Marulas (page 3) can indicate early settlements, as it was sacred to many tribes, and highly prized for its uses. The young plants would have been nurtured, and the trees would have been protected from fire and from being chopped down.

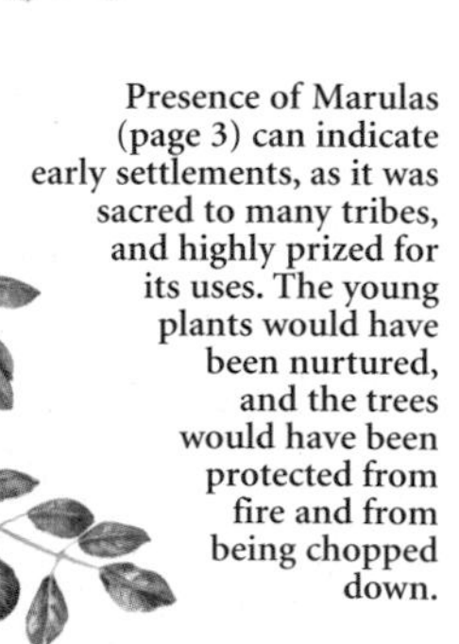

Trading and European Settlement

In recent centuries, the Mpumalanga Lowveld did not lend itself to easy exploration or settlement. Dense bush, intense heat, malaria-carrying mosquitoes and the ubiquitous tsetse fly, along with wild predators, made this a challenging frontier for even hardened and experienced foreign travellers. It was the breakaway Voortrekkers from the Cape Colony who eventually displaced the indigenous people, claimed the land and settled in much of the Lowveld.

Glass beads

Trade

Many believe mistakenly, that international trade in southern Africa began with the arrival of the Europeans. Trade in the area was, however, taking place 1 000s of years before the Europeans arrived in the mid 1800s. Later, the Lowveld attracted Arab traders from seaports on the east African coast. They came in search of 'white gold' – elephant ivory, and in the later Iron Age, 'black gold'– slave labour. Trade in iron artefacts, glass beads, ivory, bronze, gold and copper, gave rise to sophisticated societies, and inland trade centres, such as Great Zimbabwe and Mapungubwe. In the Lowveld, there are stone ruins of such centres at Thulamela, and Matevekvhele near Punda Maria. At Masorini near Phalaborwa, iron tools and weapons were manufactured well into the 19th Century.

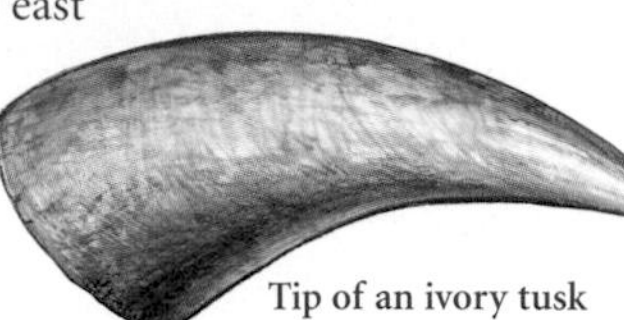

Tip of an ivory tusk

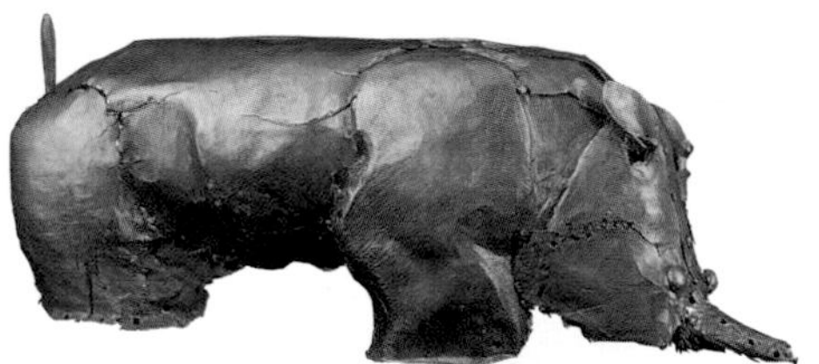

Late Iron Age rhino statue

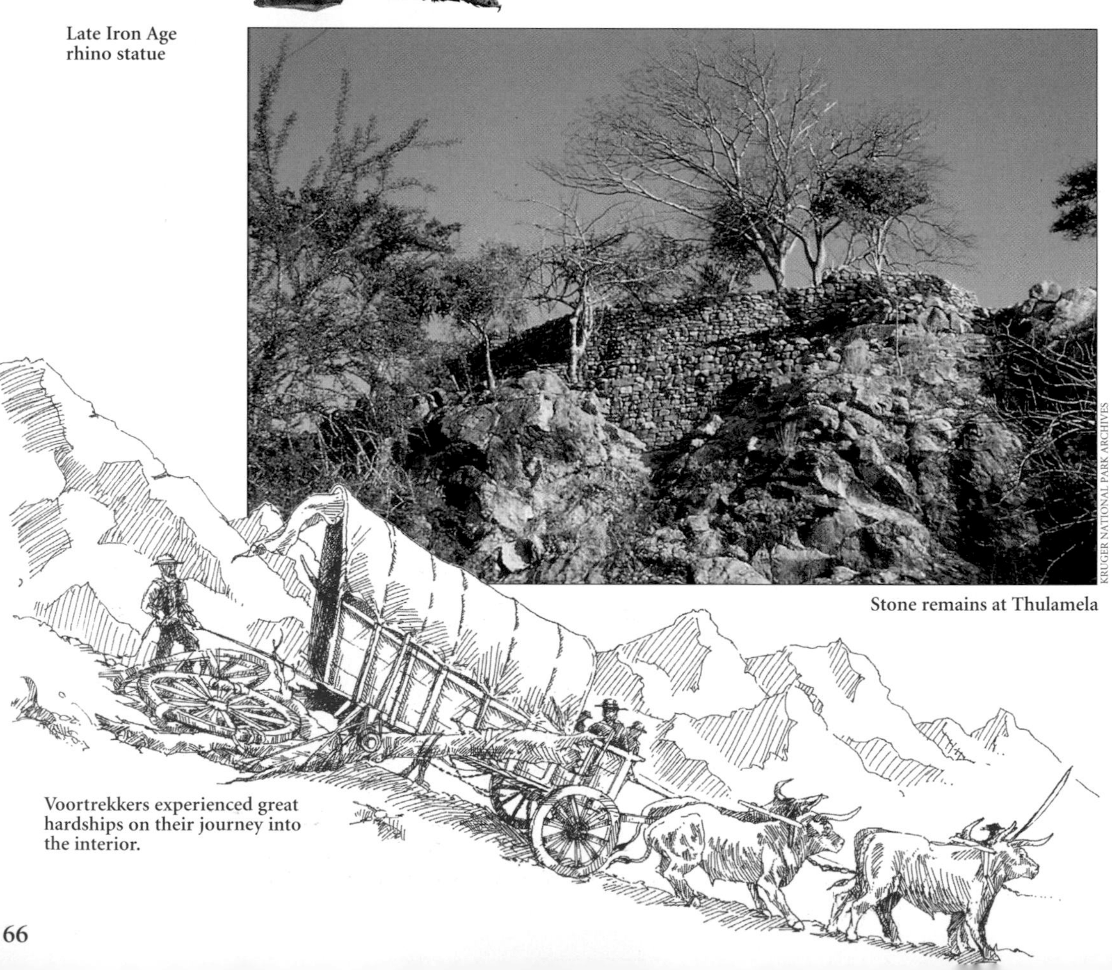

KRUGER NATIONAL PARK ARCHIVES

Stone remains at Thulamela

Voortrekkers experienced great hardships on their journey into the interior.

MUSEUM AFRICA

Broken axle on oxwagon – and 90 miles from nearest blacksmith!

Devil's Thorn (*Dicerocaryum eriocarpum*) was used for soap and shampoo.

An example of the toys made by Voortrekkers: a wagon (jaw bone) and oxen (knuckle bones)

European Settlement

The consolidation of British rule over the Cape Colony in 1806, the subsequent introduction of high taxation, and the abolition of slavery in 1835, created much resentment among the Dutch settlers in the Colony. This (and other factors) resulted in what is today known as the Great Trek. Some 5 000 people set out on the arduous journey to frontiers north of the Orange River, in hopes of establishing separate Voortrekker Republics.

Among the areas that were eventually sparsely settled by these Dutch farmers (Boers) was what is today known as the Mpumalanga Lowveld. For the Boers to escape goverment by the British, it was imperative for them to find an east coast port independent of Port Natal and Cape Town. In the process, these pioneers came up against the perils of the unforgiving environment, known as 'the white man's grave', because so many Europeans had died while attempting to explore it. Life-threatening insects, wild animals, crocodile-infested rivers, and rough and treacherous terrain decimated most groups of travellers and settlers. Records describe some of the perils they faced:

"As we penetrated deeper into the Lowveld our animals suffered grievously from tsetse fly, mosquitoes and ticks. At night, lions prowled the darkness around the camp, shattering the stillness with their roaring, and carried off much of the stock".

Against all odds, Voortrekkers, led by the likes of Andries Potgieter succeeded in surviving, displacing the Africans, and claimimg much of the interior for European settlement.

As its name indicates, Wild Cotton (*Gossypium herbaceum*) was used to make cotton.

MERVYN LOTTER

Long Tom Pass (as it looks today) was one of many passes that the Voortrekkers had to negotiate with their oxwagons.

Gold Rush

The discovery of gold in the Lowveld brought a temporary boom to the area. From 1873, hordes of fortune-seeking prospectors descended on places such as Barberton and Pilgrim's Rest to pan the rivers and excavate the reefs for gold. For a time the district was a hive of activity.

Barberton

Barberton in particular, enjoyed a lively existence as a centre of wild mining speculation, gambling and frenetic nightlife. Canteens, music halls and liquor shops competed with the mines for the biggest profits. At the height of its boom, two stock exchanges traded around the clock in the town. On the Sheba Ridge overlooking Barberton lie the ruins of one of the many digging towns – Eureka City. These diggings produced some of the highest yields in the history of gold mining – over 500 000 ounces in ten years.

Shovel used for digging gold

Miner's Lamp

Barberton cableway carrying gold from the diggings

Further north and earlier, African prospectors had been mining copper and iron in the remains of an ancient volcanic shaft. This 19^2 km area also contained such minerals as phosphates, zinc, mica and gold. The prospectors named the place Phalaborwa ('better than the south') because it was healthier than the fever-ridden areas in the south.

Gold nuggets

Fortune-seekers of the late 1800s, digging and panning for gold

Life in Pilgrim's Rest in the late 1800s

Kiaat Bloodwood (Wild Teak/Kiaat) (*Pterocarpus angolensis*) was used for timber.

The Lowveld goldrush brought an assortment of unusual characters to the area. Hunters, ivory poachers, prospectors and transport riders abounded, each hoping to profit from the discovery of gold. Men such as Sir Percy FitzPatrick (later a statesman and politician) and his transport riders, carried supplies from the east coast through tsetse fly-infested bush to the gold-digging areas of the Lowveld.

"They travelled through the worst areas at night, when the fly was less active. They smeared their draught animals with grease and potent mixtures ... and used exotic creatures such as camels in the vain hope that they would prove resistant to the disease."

With the discovery of vast gold deposits on the Witwatersrand in the late 1800s, most prospectors left the Lowveld, and the mining industry in the area collapsed. The demand for wood for the Highveld mines, was, however, to create the next boom industry. Forestry along with fruit farming has been the economic mainstay of the area ever since.

A saw from the early forestry industry

A trading store of the past, which can be visited today

Conservation

The history of the greater Kruger National Park and surrounding reserves is a story of the perseverance of many individuals and the public at large.

The Kruger Park has led the way in developing one of the finest national parks in the world, with a globally respected conservation policy.

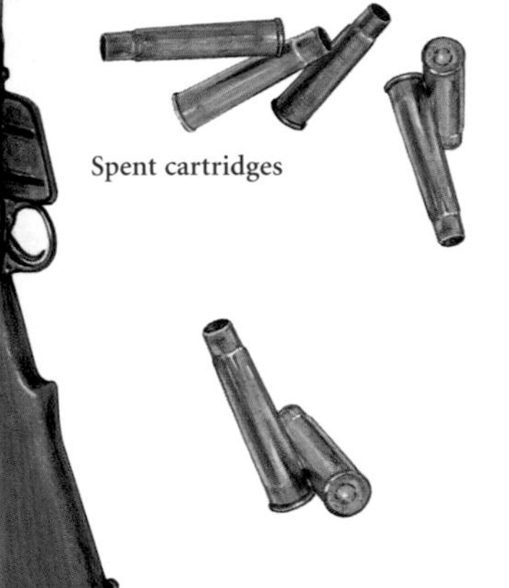

Lee-Enfield .303 rifle used by game hunters during past centuries

Spent cartridges

Hunters' Paradise

As far back as the 1860s, the Lowveld area attracted big-game hunters, particularly in the dry winter season when the threat of mosquito and tsetse fly diminished. Over the next several decades, the lure of ivory, meat, hides and hunting trophies led to the steady decline of wildlife in the area.

Mosquito (Family *Anophelinae)* played a significant role in 'keeping the Lowveld relatively pristine' as they were one of the few deterrents to European settlement.

One observer wrote at this time that, *"if sportsmen want to 'do' Africa, they had better make haste, as at the present rate of decrease, in a very few years* (wild animals*) will have ceased to exist in this territory".*

Long before the turn of the 19th Century, the quagga had been hunted into extinction in the Cape and Natal. The protection of this species was only legislated in Natal in 1886, three years after the last animal had died in a zoo in Europe. Giraffe were also hunted in large numbers, their hides used for 'riems' (thongs), to span the oxen that drove the most popular form of transport at the time – the wagon.

MUSEUM AFRICA

Hunters and their spoils, 1800s

Large-scale hunting continued unabated until the late 1800s. The few conservation laws in place, in the various small competing Republics in the Transvaal did not protect any species, but rather restricted the number of people permitted to hunt. This had grave consequences for the subsistence of indigenous hunters in the area, who were suddenly considered poachers under the law.

Survival of the fittest

In the 1890s, there was general concern over the destruction of wildlife in the Transvaal. Particularly outspoken were the sport-hunters on the goldmines in the Lowveld, who prodded the Transvaal Government into establishing a small game sanctuary in their area. Little else was achieved, however, because of the political upheavals between Boer and British over the next decade.

In the mid-1890s, the area between the Sabie and Crocodile rivers was identified as being suitable for game preservation, as malaria and tsetse fly prevented sustained human settlement. The Sabi Game Reserve was proclaimed as a Government Game Reserve in 1895, but the outbreak of the Anglo-Boer South African War in 1899 distracted the attention of legislators, and hunting continued in the area.

Stuffed heads of animals were admired as trophies in the last few centuries.

Railway Linkage

The Selati Railway line was built to serve the goldfields of the Eastern Transvaal, including Selati. Many years after the collapse of the mining of alluvial gold, the line was abandoned. It was only resuscitated after Union, in 1902, when money was made available by the Transvaal Province for agricultural needs in the centres near Pietersburg (now Polokwane). By then, there was enough traffic to justify the existence of the railway.

The first reserve and forced removals

After the Anglo-Boer South Africa War, the British victors re-proclaimed the Sabi Game Reserve, between the Sabie and Crocodile rivers, and set about clearing the way for its effective existence. This involved the forced removal of local inhabitants from the south, and in 1903, between 2000 – 3000 people were translocated out of the reserve area. Similar removals were conducted sporadically throughout Kruger's history. In 1969, after many years of dispute during the harsh apartheid era, the Makuleke people were expelled from Pafuri. Land claims today continue the tussle between the need to make restitution for unjust and forced removals, and the wide-spread advantages of maintaining a profitable and important National Park.

STEVENSON-HAMILTON COLLECTION

James Stevenson-Hamilton as a young man

Major James Stevenson-Hamilton was appointed as the first warden for the Sabi Game Reserve. The short-statured, short-tempered Scotsman earned himself the name 'Skukuza', meaning 'he who turns things upside down' or 'he who sweeps clean!' The name referred to his role in the eviction of the people living between the Crocodile and Sabie rivers. Stevenson-Hamilton set about trying to have an enlarged area officially proclaimed a wildlife reserve, and engaged in negotiations with the various individuals and mining companies who owned vast tracts of land for speculative purposes. He successfully expanded the small reserve northwards, and was given authority over the Singwitsi Game Reserve between the Luvuvhu and Letaba rivers. This area was proclaimed in 1903.

After Union, local farmers voiced stiff opposition, accusing the Reserve of being a 'breeding ground for lions'. Both domestic stock and people were often attacked, as men like Harry Wolhuter could testify. Possibly South Africa's most famous ranger, he was brought down by lions in 1903. As the big male dragged him off, he felt for its heart and stabbed it fatally with his hunting knife. Plaques have been placed at varous sites relating to this history (see page 102).

MUSEUM AFRICA

The opening of the Selati railway marked the beginning of a new social era in the Lowveld.

Kruger National Park

Over thousands of years, people have lived in what is now called the Kruger National Park. They did not significantly alter the environment so that today we can imagine what life was like for human beings in the distant past. It must have been a tougher existence than ours.

Both the climate and the prevalence of endemic diseases have changed over the centuries, but only after the rinderpest of 1895-96 had destroyed the tsetse fly, did permanent settlement become possible.

Our relationship with nature deteriorated from one of co-existence to destruction and abuse. Recently, however, Bio-diversity Conservation has become a significant force. Today, we face the challenges of the present to determine the future, but we do this with sound knowledge of the past.

Protection of Game

In the 1920s, a 9-day rail tour of South Africa was started. The most popular part of the tour proved to be the gameviewing and a night under the stars at present-day Skukuza. The fact that people would pay to see game, and not just shoot it, was proof to the politicians that transforming the various Eastern Transvaal Game Reserves into a National Park would be successful and profitable.

STEVENSON-HAMILTON ARCHIVES

An early visitor to Kruger shows the same interest in the Big Five as the tourist of the 21st Century.

In 1926, after a long-standing campaign waged by Warden Stevenson-Hamilton, with the support of a number of politicians, sport-hunters and wildlife protectionists, the National Parks Act was passed unanimously by both houses of Parliament. For the first time, tourists were allowed into the Kruger National Park.

In 1927 only three cars entered, but by two years later, there were 850 cars during the winter months when malaria was relatively dormant.

Over the next 50 years an average of some 150 000 people visited the Kruger National Park annually. Today, there are close on one million wildlife enthusiasts who enjoy the fruits of a long, fascinating and hard-won battle to create one of the finest National Parks in the world.

Private landowners, like Eileen Orpen, with her love of wildlife, donated land to the Park, increasing its size. The protection of all wildlife within the Park and the development of tourism, became official policy and the road forward was clear.

Early wardens ranged over their territory on horseback.

Archaeological Findings

Although South Africa's National Parks legislation gives equal standing to cultural and scientific research, the former has been neglected since 1926. This is at last being redressed.

In Kruger, archaeologists have identified different periods by the different types of pottery found in the area. So far, more than 12 cultural groups have been recognised, dating back to 1800 BP. Each piece of pottery is a fingerprint of a specific time and group. Beautiful, fluted, clay vessels have been found near Mopane Camp (in Kruger) and at Silver Leaves, a farm close to Tzaneen. This is the earliest archaeological record of the first farmers in South Africa. These vessels show the fine craftsmanship of the period close on 2 000 years ago. At that time, pottery was made by men, but women later adopted this role.

CHRISTO VAN DER LINDE

Restoration of sites is ongoing throughout the Lowveld including the Kruger National Park.

Honouring the Past

KRUGER NATIONAL PARK ARCHIVES

Pottery is a useful method of identifying the people who lived in an area in earlier times.

For many years, the Masorini Ruins near Phalaborwa Gate (in Kruger), have been a favourite attraction with replicas of traditional homes, as well as a genuine iron smelting site. A guide shows visitors around, and the lifestyle of the early Shangaan people and their method of mining, are explained.

More recently, Thulamela near Punda Maria was reconstructed as the start of a new era in developing sites of national interest. Over the last decade, SANParks has made a concerted effort to research areas of human history that fall within the boundaries of the Park, and to make these accessible to visitors. This is in accordance with laws for the care and reconstruction of heritage sites in South Africa.

Other sites of interest that fall within the Kruger area are listed on page 102 of the Grids.

Sacred Coral-tree leaf, flower and pod

Sacred Coral-trees (*Erythrina lysistemon*) have played an important part in the human history of the area for thousands of years.

KRUGER NATIONAL PARK ARCHIVES

The Stevenson-Hamilton library in Skukuza houses fascinating historical information for visitors to enjoy.

Lowveld Activity Grids, Maps and Index

The Lowveld!

The name conjures up adventure, fun and the best that wild Africa has to offer, with both sophisticated and rugged destinations you never dreamed were possible.

From abseiling to tubing, helicopters to quadbikes or horses and elephants, the choice of transport is yours, all heading through the untold majesty that is the Lowveld.

The following pages are as comprehensive as possible at time of print, but as tourism development blossoms in the area, new vistas and possibilities are always opening up. But in here you'll find an intriguing glimpse into some of the world's foremost eco-destinations.

Eco-sensitive Quad-biking is a wonderful way to see the country-side at close quarters. A grid with contact numbers is on page 83.

GOLDEN MONKEY

PLACES TO VISIT AND THINGS TO DO

The Lowveld is an eco-tourist paradise – a world-class destination. The listings here are to help you make the most of your experience. The colour codes refer to the **borders** around the maps on pages 104 to 111, allowing quick easy indentificaion of the area you are visiting.

KEY TO MAP COLOURS

Map	Colour
Map 1 See pages 104-105	
Map 2 See pages 106-107	
Map 3 See pages 108-109	
Map 4 See pages 110-111	

CONTENTS

Herringbone Grass
(Pognarthria squarrosa)

INFORMATION CENTRES and SERVICES

NAME	*MAP REF*	*LOCATION*	*TEL NO*
Musina Tourism Info	A1	Musina	015 534 3500
Zoutpansberg Tourism & Marketing Association	D1	Makhado (Louis Trichardt)	015516 0040
African Ivory Route Reservations	J4	Phalaborwa	015 295 3025
Limpopo Tourism	M3	Hoedspruit	014 736 4328
Phalaborwa Tourism Info	J4	Phalaborwa	015 781 7267
Valley of the Olifants Resource Centre	L2	Tzaneen	015 307 3582
Barberton Tourism	U4	Barberton	013 712 5055
Golden Monkey Reservations & Info	R4	Hazyview	013 737 8191
Hazyview Tourism	R4	Hazyview	013 737 7414
Komatipoort Tourism	S7	Komatipoort	013 793 7218
Kruger Park Reservations	R4	Hazyview	013 737 7308
Lowveld Environmental Services	T3	Nelspruit	013 744 7216
Lowveld Tourism	T3 S4	Nelspruit White River	013 755 1988 013 750 1073
Mainline Train Services	T5	Nelspruit	013 752 9257
Malelane Information	T5	Malelane	013 790 1193
Mpumalanga Parks Board	T3	Nelspruit	013 759 5300
Mpumalanga Tourism	T3	Nelspruit	013 752 7001
Nelspruit Tourism	T3	Nelspruit	013 755 1988
Sabie Tourism	R3	Sabie	013 764 1125
Trips SA	R4	Hazyview	013 764 1177
Discovering SA Hotline	–	Cape Town	083 123 2345

EMERGENCY SERVICES

NAME	*TEL NO*
Automobile Association	
Roadside Assistance	0800 010101
Medical Rescue	0800 033007
Directory Enquiries	1023
Fire Brigade	013 753 3331
Highway Patrol Nelspruit	013 750 0888
Mcare:	
Ambulance	083 292 1607
Emergency Services	083 292 1607
Netcare 911:	
Ambulance Service	082 911
Medical Rescue	082 911
Police – Emergency Service	10111
Poison Info Centre	0800 333444
Weather Bureau	082 233 9800

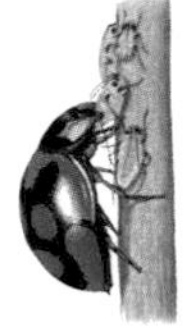

Ladybird
(page vi)

- **Please note that telephone numbers do change.**
- **For further information or clarification, consult the local telephone directories, or contact 1023 for directory assistance.**
- **The publishers welcome feedback from readers.**

TRANSPORT and TRAVEL

NAME	MAP REF	AREA	TEL NO	COMMENTS
City Bug	T3	Nelspruit	013 741 4114	Taxi service from airport; booking and payment in advance
Greyhound	T3	Nelspruit	013 753 2100	Regular bus service between Johannesburg and Nelspruit
Information Desk	S4	KMI Airport *	013 753 7500	General Information
Lowveld Link	S4	White River	013 750 1174	Shuttle service (16-seater bus) between White River, Nelspruit, Pretoria, Johannesburg
NAC Charter Service	T3	Nelspruit	013 741 4838	Air charters; bases throughout Africa
Nelair Charters	T3	Nelspruit	013 741 2012	Air charters throughout southern Africa
SA Airlink	S4	KMI Airport *	013 750 2531	Regular flights to Johannesburg; one flight daily
SA Express	S4	KMI Airport *	013 750 2531	Regular flights to Johannesburg; one flight to Durban daily
Tamboti Tours	S4	White River	082 451 8149	Saloon car and 11-seater bus; airport shuttle service transfers; booking in advance, payment on arrival
* KMI Airport – Kruger Mpumalanga International Airport, White River - see below				

Black-breasted Snake Eagle *(Circaetus pectoralis)*

TRAIN EXCURSIONS

CONTACT	TEL NO	COMMENTS
Bushveld Train Safaris	014 736 3025 082 920 7576	Wide choice of excursions available throughout South Africa; numerous safaris through Lowveld area departing Pretoria or Johannesburg; various trips: 2 nights – 11 days
Rovos Rail	012 323 6052	Numerous exciting trips throughout South Africa; Lowveld trip includes Nelspruit, Kruger Park, Dullstroom, Wild Dog and Cheetah Research Centre; boma lunch; departs private station Pretoria once weekly; charters arranged

Peeling Plane Ochna *(Ochna pulchra)*

SA RAILWAYS

South African Railways train

AIRPORTS

NAME	MAP REF	AREA	TEL NO	TYPE
Makhado	D1	Makhado/ Louis Trichardt	015 516 0212	Landing strip only
Phalaborwa Airport	J4	Phalaborwa	015 781 5823 015 781 5833	Private airport – belongs to S A Airlink
Hoedspruit Eastgate	M3	Hoedspruit	015 793 3681 015 793 3091	Private airport; 2 flights daily from Johannesburg, 1 from Cape Town; small charters
Nelspruit Aerodrome	T3	Nelspruit	013 741 3636	Charters only
KMI Airport*	S4	Plaston	013 753 7500	8 daily flights from and to Johannesburg, 1 from Durban, 1 from Cape Town; private and commercial charters, some from Maputo; car rentals; customs and immigration; Kruger Park information center; curio and jewellery shops; restaurant

VEHICLE HIRE

Comb Duck
(Knob-billed Duck)
(Sarkidiornis melanotos)

NAME	MAP REF	AREA	TEL NO	TYPE
Avis	M3	Hoedspruit	015 793 2014	Economy class; luxury vehicles; 4X4; 10-seater buses
Avis	S4	KMI Airport *	013 750 1015	Economy class; luxury vehicles
Budget Rent-a-Car	S4	KMI Airport *	013 751 1774	Economy class; Microbuses; 4X4
Europcar	S4	KMI Airport *	013 750 0965	Economy class; Microbuses; 4X4
Imperial	S4	KMI Airport *	013 750 2871	Economy class; Microbuses; 4X4
National	S4	KMI Airport *	013 750 2538	Economy class; luxury vehicles; utility vehicles; 11- to 16-seater buses; 4X4
Tempest	T3	Nelspruit	013 755 3483	Economy class; 11-seater buses; utility vehicles; 4X4
Untamed	Q6	Skukuza	013 735 5701	Landrover; 4X4

* KMI Airport – Kruger Mpumalanga International Airport, White River - see page 79

TOUR OPERATORS

NAME	MAP REF	AREA	TEL NO	COMMENTS
Action Travel	J4	Phalaborwa	015 781 1188	SATOUR registered; owner-guided tours of Lowveld and entire South Africa; hunting and conservation excursions
Phalaborwa Gate Safaris	J4	Phalaborwa	015 781 0027	Guided night drives; bush braais; guided walks into Kruger
Sure Turn Key Travel Tours & Safaris	J4 R4	Phalaborwa Hazyview	015 781 2492 013 737 6837 082 428 8223	Travel agent; book for safaris and activities at Elephant Herd Adventure centre; half- and full-day open vehicle tours; night drives; transfers
Africa Sepungu	M3	Hoedspruit	013 737 6871	Day and night safaris; tours to White Lions and Cheetah Research
Blyde Canyon Adventure	M3	Hoedspruit	015 793 0426	White-water rafting and boat trips on Blyde River and Olifants River
Kruger Safari & Adventure Company	M3	Hoedspruit	013 737 7115	Adventure activities; ballooning; 4X4; helicopter flights
McFarlane Safaris	M3	Hoedspruit	015 793 3000	Calabash of cultures; bush and beach package in Kruger and Mozambique; white-knuckle adventure
Nsele Safaris	M3	Hoedspruit	015 793 2443	Comprehensive tour to Kruger and numerous wildlife, eco- and cultural destinations
Safari Plans	M3	Hoedspruit	015 795 5054	Predominantly inbound; tailor-made tours; fly and drive to all lodges and Kruger; will suit any needs
Viva Safaris	M3	Hoedspruit	011 476 8842	Transfers from Johannesburg and Pretoria to Tremisana Game Lodge and Marks Tree House Camp in Hoedspruit
Emoyeni Lodge & Tours	T3	Nelspruit	013 744 9551 082 576 5214	Guided, luxury, 1- to 24-day tours of Lowveld and other southern African eco-destinations
Getaway Tours	T5	Malelane	013 790 0609	Safaris into Kruger, Lebombo Eco-Trail and Phandinani Rhino Reserve
Golden Monkey	R4	Hazyview	013 737 8191	Booking agents for activity-tourism; horse trails, quad biking, hiking, ballooning; local and long-distance panoramic transfers

Tree Wisteria
(Bolusanthus speciosus)

Ants
Family Formicidae

TOUR OPERATORS (Continued)

NAME	*MAP REF*	*AREA*	*TEL NO*	*COMMENTS*
Untamed	Q6	Skukuza	013 735 5701	Based at Skukuza inside Kruger Park; guided Kruger safaris; game tracking by experienced rangers
Green Rhino	S4	White River	013 751 1952	Covers entire southern Africa region; tours and itineraries
Induna Adventures	R4	Hazyview	013 737 8308	Adventure activities; quad bikes; horse trails; abseiling; mountain biking; sun-downer at Dagama Dam
Katambora Safari	S4	White River	013 751 3339	Youth camps; adult and junior ranger training courses offered; conference facilities; guided walks on private Big 5 Reserves
Lalela Backpackers	T3	Nelspruit	013 751 2812	Backpackers and B&B facilities. 1-day to 3-week trips; will cater for specific tour requests
Lawson's Tours	T3	Nelspruit	013 741 2458	Birdwatching safaris 1-day to 3-week trips
Lowveld Enviro Services	T3	Nelspruit	013 744 7043	Open-vehicle Kruger Safaris; booking office at Malelane Sun
Mac Rob Safaris	T3	Nelspruit	013 750 1782	Self-catering establishment; on-site guide for specific services
Matthew Greeff Safaris	T3	Nelspruit	013 744 0355	International clientele; photographic and hunting safaris; taxidermy services through Lifeform in White River
Mfafa Safaris	S4	White River	013 750 1782	Tailor-made safaris; will do anything physically possible to meet your needs
Place of Rock Tours & Safaris	R4	Hazyview	013 737 7265	Open vehicle full- or 1/2-day drives in Kruger; bush walks in Sabie and Kapama; tours to Rehabilitation Centre
Safarilandia	T3	Nelspruit	082 338 9055	Weekend tiger-fishing; quad-bike safaris; open vehicle 1-day to 3-night excursions into the parks
Safaris Direct	R4	Hazyview	013 737 7945	Guided game drives in Kruger; panoramic drives
Solitaire Tours & Safaris	T3	Nelspruit	013 752 4527	Open-vehicle drives in Kruger, Mpumalanga; escarpment day-tours; group bookings
Sure Turn Key Travel Tours & Safaris	R4	Hazyview	013 737 6837 082 428 8223	Travel agent; book for safaris and activities at Elephant Herd Adventure centre; half- and full-day open vehicle tours; night drives; transfers
Thompson's Indaba Safaris	R4	Hazyview	013 737 7115	Transfers; night safaris into Kruger; adventure tours; panoramic tours
Tour d'Afrique	S4	White River	013 750 1107	Conference and coach charters throughout South Africa; open-vehicle game drives in Kruger and private reserves
Vula Tours	T3	Nelspruit	013 741 2826	Open-vehicle safaris in Kruger
McFarlane Safaris		Hoedspruit	015 793 3000	Various tours to suit requirements

Rhinocerus Beetle
(page 24, 25)

GOLDEN MONKEY

Tours in open vehicles are a feature of many exciting excursions.

Apricot Playboy Butterfly (page xv)

GOLDEN MONKEY

A helicopter ride gives a great perspective of the western mountains dropping sharply to the eastern Lowveld.

African Leopard Butterfly (page 12)

Fig-tree Blue Butterfly (page xx)

TOURS

NAME	*MAP REF*	*AREA*	*TEL NO*	*INFORMATION*
Bergpan Salt Mine Tour	D1	Vivo	015 593 0127 015 593 0107	Tour through salt mine and how Africans farmed; self-hike to San rock art
Venetia Diamond Mine Tour	A1	Musina	015 516 9100	Largest production diamond mine in RSA; book 2 weeks in advance; min 5 people per tour; 3 hour tour to pit and various mining areas and diamond display room
Cultural Excursion Tour	J4	Phalaborwa	015 781 7267	Tour of townships, Phalaborwa town and mining areas; river cruises on the Olifants River
Foskor Mine	J4	Phalaborwa	015 789 2024	Open-cast mineral mine: tours must be booked in advance
Bombyx More	M3	Hoedspruit	015 795 5813	Fascinating tour of entire silk-production process: exclusive silk goods can be purchased; silkworm population varies from 50 000 to 250 000
Andante Farm	S4	White River	013 751 3059	Goats' milk cheese tours; by appointment only; special treat for children
Birdlife Lowveld	T3	Nelspruit	013 753 3238	Maps and instructions are given to visiting birders; birders can join organised outings by special arrangement
Coffee Farm Tours	R4	Hazyview	013 737 8191	Entire process, from orchards to roasting and packaging; sample various coffee roasts and delicious cakes (incl); Mon-Wed 14h30-17h15, Sat 09h30-12h15
Croc River Environ Park	T3	Nelspruit	013 752 5511	Tour Reptile Park; live demonstrations; daily 09h00 and 15h00
De Bruge Ostrich Farm	U4	Barberton	013 712 5265	Tour Ostrich Farm; daily at 10h00
Eureka City Tour	U4	Barberton	013 737 8191	Visit lost city ruins and experience history of 1880 pioneers; go underground into gold mine; discover Cradle of Life; picnic lunches in the mountains
Hops Hollow Brewery	R3	Sabie	013 235 2275	Learn about this smallest brewery in South Africa while tasting locally brewed beers with historically linked names: Diggers Draught and Mac's Porter
Nabana Park	R4	Hazyview	013 737 8026	Banana plantation tour, including birdlife and fauna

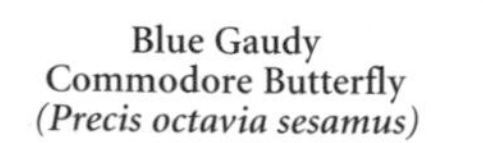

Blue Gaudy Commodore Butterfly *(Precis octavia sesamus)*

TOURS (continued)

NAME	MAP REF	AREA	TEL NO	INFORMATION
Africa Silks	P3	Graskop	013 767 1665	Tour factory in Graskop where silk from Silkworms and Mopani Worms is processed; silk weaving also demonstrated
Gold Panning	P3	Pilgrim's Rest	013 737 8191	Tour will demonstrate how prospectors panned for gold – try it yourself; receive certificate and 'gold dust'; complementary drinks
Phumelani Cultural Experience	R4	Hazyview - Numbi Gate	013 798 0020	African cultural performance - Mdluli tribe performs for groups; includes buffet meal
Research Institute – Tropical & Sub-tropical fruit	T3	Nelspruit	013 753 7000	Agricultural tour covers laboratories, nursery and previous century farming implements
Rottcher Wineries	T3	Nelspruit	013 751 3884	Tour of orange and ginger winery and macadamia nut farm; daily tours 10h00 and 14h00
Shangana Cultural Village	R4	Hazyview	013 737 7000	Authentic African village - homes of descendants of Chief Shoshangana; 1-hour tours through village; lunch time or evening tours – traditional meal
Tsinini Silk Farm	R4	Hazyview	013 767 1665	Tour silkworm farm, watch weaving of silk from cocoons to make silk articles

GOLDEN MONKEY

There are numerous tours to watch weavers at work and buy unique local product

Guineafowl Butterfly (page v)

MAJOR ANNUAL and SPORTING EVENTS

Bushveld Charaxes Butterfly *(Cymothoe coranus)*

EVENT	MAP REF	AREA	DATES	COMMENTS
Birding Big Day		Southern Africa	November	Annual; teams of 3 or 4 Birders collect and pay sponsorship money for Conservation projects; contact Birdlife SA 011 7891122
Kruger Park Half Marathon	Q6	Skukuza	August	Run annually by Kruger Marathon Club; limited to 1 000 runners who raise money for Conservation projects; run through and around Skukuza village and golf course
Lowveld Airshow	T3	Nelspruit	June	Aviation expo at Old Nelspruit Airport; civilian and military aircraft; flying and tatic displays
Lowveld Show	T3	Nelspruit	August	Annual expo of commerce, industry, agriculture and tourism in the Lowveld
Sasol Area	T3	Nelspruit	Around 20 June	Annual national event, affiliated to Motor-Rally sport SA, in Nelspruit, Sabie, White River

BOATING, CRUISING and FISHING

CONTACT	MAP REF	AREA	TEL NO	COMMENTS
Jumbo River Safaris	J4	Phalaborwa	015 781 6168	Boating and cruising; sunrise excursions; full moon/sunset cruises through Klaserie Big 5 Game Reserve; self-cater or catered; sleep on board or riverside accommodation available Hulala Lakeside Lodge
Canyon Adventure	M3	Hoedspruit	015 793 0426	Boating and cruising; white-water rafting and boat trips on Blyde and Olifants rivers
Hulala Lakeside Lodge	S4	White River	013 764 1893	Bass fishing
Sundowner Cruises	S4	Dagama Dam	013 737 8191	Boating and cruising; 2-hour trip on Dagama Dam; cruise includes snacks and cash bar

Common Water Snake *(Lycodonomorphus rufulus)* with Common River Frog *(Afrana angolensis)*

TUBING and RIVER RAFTING

CONTACT	MAP REF	AREA	TEL NO	COMMENTS
Golden Monkey	R3	Sabie	013 737 8191	Tubing excursions organised to Sabie River
Hardy Ventures	R4	Hazyview	013 751 1693	River rafting; 2-hour trips on local rivers using 'Crocodiles'
Riverwild	T3	Nelspruit	013 733 3366	River rafting and tubing (seasonal) on Houtbosloop River
Sabie River	R4	Hazyview	013 737 8191	River rafting and swimming – Sabie River

Tadpoles

GOLDEN MONKEY

White-water- and River-rafting are activities in the south-western areas

ABSEILING and CAVING

CONTACT	MAP REF	AREA	TEL NO	COMMENTS
Adventure Centre	R3 & R4	Hazyview & Sabie	013 737 8191	Abseiling and caving; book through Golden Monkey
Hardy Ventures	R3	Hazyview	013 751 1693	Abseil down 30 m granite rock
Riverwild	T3	Nelspruit	013 733 3366	Abseiling; caving in Sudwala Caves

Problem water plant - Water Hyacinth *(Eichhornia crassipes)* fills our dams and kills the wildlife.

GOLDEN MONKEY

Kloofing!

ELEPHANT and HORSE TRAILS

CONTACT	*MAP REF*	*AREA*	*TEL NO*	*COMMENTS*
Elephant-back Safaris	M3	Hoedspruit	015 793 1265	1.5 – 2 hour Safari on African Elephant saved from culling; drinks included; am & pm
Adventure Safaris	R4	Hazyview	013 737 8191	Horse riding
Golden Monkey	R4	Hazyview	013 737 8191	Variety of horseback safaris
Kaapsehoop Horse Trails	T3	Kaapse-hoop	013 734 4995 082 774 5826	For beginners or experienced riders; stay at historical mining village, ride through forest and grasslands; lead-rein: 0.5 hr – 5 days
Sabie Forest Outride	R3	Sabie	013 737 8191	Horse trail bookings through Golden Monkey
Sabie River Valley Trail	R3	Sabie	013 737 8191	Book through Golden Monkey

4X4 ADVENTURES and QUAD-BIKING

EVENT	*MAP REF*	*LOCATION*	*TEL NO*	*COMMENTS*
Jumbo River Safaris	J4	Phalaborwa	015 781 6168	To Klaserie (Big 5) Game Reserve; 2.5hr game viewing in 40-seater Uni-Mog
Kruger Safari & Adventure Company	M3	Hoedspruit	013 737 6661	Adventure activities in 4X4; ballooning and helicopter excursions
Night Safaris	P5/6	Sabi Sands Wildtuin	013 737 8191	Hotel pick-up in 4X4; late afternoon dinner in boma at private game lodge
Bush & Culture Trail	R4	Hazyview	013 737 8191	Various quad-bike excursions available
Place of Rock Tours & Safaris	R4	Hazyview	013 737 7265	Weekend quad-bike safaris
Riverwild	T3	Nelspruit	013 733 3366	4X4 driver training; trails, out-rides
Sabie River Valley Trail	R4	Hazyview	013 737 8191	Various quad-bike excursions
Safarilandia	T3	Nelspruit	082 338 9055	Quad-bike weekend safaris
Waterfall & Forest Trail	R4	Hazyview	013 737 8191	Quad-bike excursions to forest and waterfalls
Lebombo 4X4 Trail	S6/7 to A4	Komatipoort to Pafuri area	012 426 5117	'Wilderness experience on wheels;' drive entire length of Kruger Park; trail crosses escarpment, gorges, river valleys, plains; 35 different habitats; 5-days; own vehicle

Natal-mahogany flower, leaf and fruit *(Trichelia emetica)*

Crested Guineafowl *(Guttera pucherani)*

Adventure sports, like abseiling abound.

GOLDEN MONKEY

ANIMAL REHABILITATION CENTRES, BIRD PARKS and REPTILE GARDENS

CONTACT	*MAP REF*	*LOCATION*	*TEL NO*	*COMMENTS*
Hoedspruit Research & Breeding Centre	M3	Hoedspruit	015 793 1633 015 793 1825	Open-vehicle tour to see cheetah and Wild Dog
Kapama Lodge	M3	Hoedspruit	015 793 1038	Organised tours to Endangered Species Centre
Makwalo White Lion Project	M3	Guernsey Rd, Hoedspruit	015 793 2168	Tours through White Lion Breeding Project
Moholoholo Rehabilitation Centre	M3	Kampers Rus, Hoedspruit	015 795 5236	Haven for the Magnificent 7; also offers accommodation
Swadini Reptile Park	M3	Hoedspruit	015 795 5203	Research and educational facility; birdlife
Lowveld Bird Society	T3	Nelspruit	013 753 3238 013 744 9371	Speakers - 2nd Tues of month; Outings - 3rd Sun of month
Blue Swallow Bird Watching	T3	Kaapsehoop	072 340 5588	Opportunity to see endangered species in seasonal habitat; plus 140 other species
Croc River Park	S2	Nelspruit	013 752 5511	Africa's largest reptile park and Enviro animal farm; picnic, braai facilities; tea garden
De Brug Ostrich Farm	T3	Kaapsehoop	013 712 5265	Guided tour daily at 10h00

Blue Swallow *(Hirundo atrocaerulea)* are endangered, and can be seen at Kaapsehoop.

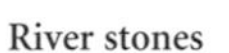

River stones

Strelitzia walk - National Botalical Gardens east of Nelspruit

Striped Mouse *(Rhabdomus pumilio)* (page xi)

BOTANICAL GARDEN and NATURE RESERVES (NR)

NAME	*MAP REF*	*AREA*	*TEL NO*	*DESCRIPTION*
Modjadji Cycad Reserve	G1	Modjadji	015 295 3025	Hiking trail amongst 800 year old Cycads and other wonderful plants and birds
Klaserie Dam NR	M4	Klaserie	015 793 2831	Fishing; camping and caravan facilities
Lowveld National Botanical Gardens	T3	Nelspruit	013 752 5531	Welcome to Paradise – extensive indigenous trees and cycads, African rainforest, waterfalls, walking trails, picnic spots, restaurant

BALLOON, HELICOPTER and FIXED-WING FLIGHTS, MICROLIGHT and PARAGLIDING

Ballooning is a wonderful way to see the sights.

Golden Monkey

CONTACT	MAP REF	AREA	TEL NO	COMMENTS
Kruger Safari & Adventure Company	M3	Hoedspruit	013 737 6661	Fixed-wing flights; ballooning; adventure excursion activities; helicopter flights
McFarlane Safaris	M3	Hoedspruit	015 793 3000	Helicopter sightseeing flights; airport transfers
Adventure Centre	R4	Hazyview	013 737 8191	Ballooning – experience romance and grace of oldest form of human flight
Balloons over Africa	R4	Hazyview	013 752 5265	Early morning ballooning; champagne-breakfast flights
Lowveld Slope Soaring Club	T3	Nelspruit	013 741 2133 082 966 2047	Para-gliding instruction and tandem flights available; weekends, holidays only
National Airways Corporation	T3	Nelspruit	013 741 4650	Fixed-wing and helicopter flights – scenic trips over Blyde River area, Graskop, Mac Mac Falls, Lisbon and Berlyn Falls, God's Window; transfers to lodges
Nelair Charters	T3	Nelspruit	013 741 2012	Fixed-wing flights – scenic Lowveld flights; from/to any airstrip in area
Pyramid Flying School	U4	Barberton	013 744 8248 082 337 8206	Microlight training and scenic flights over the Lowveld; game-viewing flights; micro-light safaris
Sabie Valley View Excursions	R4	Hazyview	013 737 8191	Helicopter and microlight flights over Sabie River Valley; eagle's view of Dagama Dam
Sabie Valley Flip	R3	Sabie	013 737 8191	Microlight excursions; book various flights through Golden Monkey
The Fabulous Falls Flip	R4	Hazyview	013 737 8191	Helicopter flights over Graskop to Pinnacle – view of Falls and God's Window

Please note that telephone numbers do change. For further information or clarification, consult the local telephone directories, or contact 1023 for directory assistance. The publishers welcome feedback from readers of these pages.

GOLF

NAME	MAP REF	AREA	TEL NO	OB	PW	DO	TO	PS	OTHER INFO
Hans Merensky Estate Gold	J4	Phalaborwa	015 781 3931	Private	Yes	7	07h00	Yes	18 hole; wild-life on course
Skukuza Golf Club	Q6	Skukuza	013 735 5543	Parks Board	Yes	7	07h00	Yes	18-hole; sponsor competition Sat
Barberton Golf Club	U4	Barberton	013 712 2923	Club	Yes	6	07h00	Yes	9-hole
Kruger Park Lodge Golf Course	R4	Hazyview	013 737 7021	Kruger Lodge	Yes	7	07h00	Yes	9-hole
Malelane Country Club	T5	Malelane	013 790 0283	Club	Yes	7	07h00	Yes	18-hole; competition Wed and Sat
Nelspruit Golf Club	T3	Nelspruit	013 752 2187	Club	Yes	7	06h30	Yes	18-hole
Pine Lake Inn Golf Club	S4	White River	013 751 5036	Private	Yes	7	06h30	No	9-hole
Sabie Country Club	R3	Sabie	013 764 2282	Private	Yes	7	07h00	Yes	18-hole; carts available
Sabie River Bungalows	R3	Sabie	013 737 7311	Private	Yes	7	07h00	Yes	18-hole; members and residents only on Sat
White River Country Club	S4	White River	013 751 3781	Private	Yes	7	07h00	Yes	18-hole; competition Wed and Sat
McFarlane Safaris (Birdies & Eagles)		Various courses	015 793 3000	–	–	–	–	–	Golf safaris to various courses according to clients' requirements

OB	Owned By
PW	Public Welcome
DO	Days Open
TO	1st Tee-off Time
PS	Pro Shop

Blue Swallow (page 84)

HIKING TRAILS – DAY EXCURSIONS

TRAIL	*MAP REF*	*AREA*	*TEL NO*	*DESCRIPTION*
African Rain Forest Trail	S3	Lowveld Botanical Gardens, Nelspruit	013 752 5531	0.5 km; 0.5 hour
Fortuna Mine Nature Trail	U4	Barberton	013 712 2121	Old Mine Tunnel, 600 m length underground; 2 km walk; 1 hour
Heritage Walk	U4	Barberton	013 712 2121	Historical walk through Barberton; 0.5 hour
Nelspruit Nature Reserve	T3	Nelspruit	013 759 9111	0.5 hour walks
Hulala Lakeside Lodge	S4 153	White River	013 764 1893	3 walks; 1.5 - 2 hours; Red, Blue, Orange Trail
Pioneer Mine	U4	Barberton	013 712 2121	Historical mining tour; 1.5 km walk; 1.5 hours
Queen Rose Hiking Trail	U4	Nelshoogte Reserve, Barberton	013 712 2247	Montrose Section: 13 km, 5-7 hours, 120 species of indigenous trees; Queens River Section: 8 km, 5 hours, 80 species of indigenous trees
Riverside Trail	T3	Lowveld Botanical Gardens, Nelspruit	013 752 5531	I km; 1 hour; not for the elderly or very young
Forest Falls	R1-P2	Sabie-Graskop	013 764 1058	4 km; 0.5 - 1 hour walk
Lourie Trails	R1	Sabie	013 764 1058	14 km; day walk
Mac Mac Pools	R3-P3	Sabie-Graskop	013 764 1058	4 km; 0.5 - 1 hour walk
Komatiland Forests Eco-tourism	Various	-	013 764 2423 013 7641392	Various 1- day hiking trails

OVERNIGHT HIKING TRAILS

TRAIL	*MAP REF*	*AREA*	*TEL NO*	*DESCRIPTION*
Prospector's HT *	P3	Graskop	012 481 3615	55 km circular route; 4 days
Fanie Botha HT *	R3	Sabie	012 481 3615	79 km circular route; 2-5 days
Kaapsehoop HT *	T3	Nelspruit	012 481 3615	66 km circular route; 2-5 days
Uitsoek HT *	T3	Nelspruit	012 481 3615	29.5 km; 2 days
Gold Nugget HT *	U4	Barberton	013 712 2121	37-44 km circular route; 2-3 days

* HT – Hiking Trail. Most of the trails mentioned here, include a wide range of short and long routes of varying difficulty.

Some of the fascinating things you may see on the hike

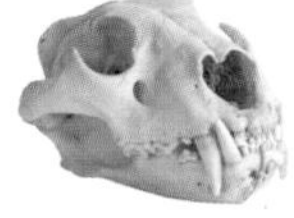

GOLDEN MONKEY

Major rivers in the Lowveld run from west to east and offer a wide variety of habitats for hikers.

OVERNIGHT GUIDED WILDERNESS TRAILS

TRAIL	MAP REF	AREA	TEL NO	DESCRIPTION
Back Packers Trails	–	Various	013 790 1280	Starting late 2003-2004; 8 persons per trail; pitch tents where convenient; trail tailored to group requirements; booking through Wilderness Company
Komatiland Forests Eco-tourism	–	Various	012 481 3615	Various hikes from 2 to 5 days duration in game reserves and historical towns

Vervet Monkey
(page 31)

Coqui Francolin *(Peliperdix coqui)* are the smallest Lowveld Francolin, but the most distinctive.

KRUGER NATIONAL PARK TRAILS

Kruger Park Trails have uniquely situated, beautiful camps.

KRUGER NATIONAL PARK – OVERNIGHT GUIDED WILDERNESS TRAILS

These areas all share Wilderness qualities of remoteness and undisturbed tranquillity. Most base camps are rustic, with A-frame huts, central ablutions and boma; all meals provided; two walks each day with armed rangers into pristine Wilderness areas with no other signs of human influence.

TRAIL	MAP REF	VICINITY	TEL NO	SIZE ha	INFORMATION
Nyalaland	B4	Pafuri – Punda Maria	012 426 5111 013 790 1480	80 000	Diverse vegetation, flowing Luvuvhu River, sandstone hills; rich in history, culture; old ruins, fossilised Dinosaurs; excellent bird sightings
Olifants	J6	Olifants River area	012 426 5111 013 790 1480	65 000	Confluence of Letaba and Olifants rivers, rugged remote Lebombo Mountains; camp next to river; waterbirds, elephant
Metsi Metsi	P7	North of Skuzuza South of Satara	012 426 5111 013 790 1480	35 000	Eastern escarpment of KNP, rugged deep valleys, Nwaswitsontso River; Hippo pools, plains game, elephant
Sweni	M7	East KNP Satara area	012 426 5111 013 790 1480	40 000	Flat plains, savannah-type habitat; camp on Sweni River; plains game, buffalo herds, ever-present lion
Bushman's	S5	South-west KNP; Malelane area	012 426 5111 013 790 1480	30 000	Deep valleys, rugged mountains, remote, typical bushveld vegetation; fantastic game; concentrations of Square-lipped Rhino, buffalo
Napi	R5	Pretoriuskop area	012 426 5111 013 790 1480	45 000	Rebuilt after 2001 fire; only luxury en suite tents on Biyamiti River; riverine trees, thick wooded areas, brackish open areas; Hook-lipped Rhino
Wolhuter	S5	South-west KNP Malelane area	012 426 5111 013 790 1480	52 000	Long beautiful valleys, rugged, mountains; great views; concentrations of Square-lipped Rhino, buffalo

Use the Maps and the Grids to enjoy your wildlife visit!

Each map is colour coded so that you can cross reference the information on these grids with the correct map.

- Each wildlife destination listed on the following pages, that is outside the official road network of the Kruger Park, is marked both on the grids and on its map with a number as well as this icon – ⌂.
- If it is inside Kruger, but a private concession, it has a number and this icon – ⌂.
- Official Kruger Camps have this icon – ⌂ or ⌂⌂ and the name of the camp, but no number.

Marula (page 8)

Here is a list of the destinations in numerical order with the page number where you will find them on a grid. There are spaces in the sequence of numbers for future editions.

Sticky Acacia *(Acacia borlea)* is an Acacia specific to the RSA Lowveld.

ECO-DESTINATION CARAVAN PARKS, CAMPING and NATURE RESERVES

Accommodation is available, at all these destinations

NAME	*MAP REF*	*AREA*	*TEL NO*	*SD*	*GD*	*SW*	*GW*	*WA*	*FACILITIES*
Modjadji – African Ivory Route Camp	G1 12	Modjadji	015 295 3025			•	•		Nature Reserve; accommodation in traditional huts; self-catering; hiking trails amongst 800-year-old cycads to kraal of Queen Modjadji; excellent for plants and birds
Aventura Swadini	M4 48	Acornhoek	015 795 5141	•		•		•	Self-catering chalets; caravan sites; electrically powered; hot and cold swimming pools; trampoline; hiking trails
Baobab Lodge	K2 16	Makalali	015 534 3504						Caravan park and camping; self-catering chalets; swimming pool
Lourene Resort	L2 17	Gravelotte	015 793 2988		•	•	•	•	Lodge with luxury accommodation-en suite; TV; open plan restaurant; B&B, caravan park; self-catering; in conservancy with Makalali and Ebeni; game drives and walks

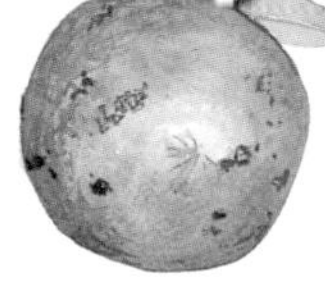

Black Monkey-orange (page 8)

Bushwillow (page 3, 5, 12)

SD	Self Drive
GD	Guided Drive
SW	Self Walk
GW	Guided Walk
WA	Wheelchair Access

Sicklebush (page 6)

ECO-DESTINATIONS BORDERING NATURE and GAME RESERVES

NAME	*MAP REF*	*AREA*	*TEL NO*	*SD*	*GD*	*SW*	*GW*	*WA**	*FACILITIES*
Cheetah Inn	M4 73	Acornhoek	015 793 1200		•		•	•	Hotel; chalets; B&B; à la carte restaurant
Protea Hotel Kruger Gate	Q6 157	Hazyview	013 735 5671		•		•	•	Hotel; B&B; full board available
Buhala Country House	S6 175	Malelane	013 792 4372	•	•		•	•	Finalists 'Best Accommodation' awards; colonial-style hotel; splendid outlook over Crocodile River; safaris into Kruger Park; golf available at Leopard Creek; day visitors welcome
Elephant Walk	S7 168	Komatipoort	015 781 2758		•		•		Backpacker s lodge; self-catering cottage; B&B
Kruger Park Lodge	R4 152	Sabie	013 737 7021		•	•		•	Self-catering chalets; à la carte restaurant
Malelane Gate Resort	T6 174	Malelane	013 790 0291		•			•	Rooms; self-catering chalets; B&B
Malelane Sun	S6 163	Malelane	011 482 3500 013 790 3304		•		•	•	Hotel; chalets; B&B; à la carte restaurant
Ngwenya Lodge	S7 167	Komatipoort	013 793 7369						Lodge bordering Kruger; time-share resort; self-walking; well located for Kruger
Pine Lake Inn	S4 154	White River	013 751 5036						Hotel and B&B on Pine Lake; 35 km from Kruger; pedal boats, canoes; 9-hole golf course
River House	T5 173	Malelane	013 790 1333		•	•	•		Rooms; optional B&B
Sabie River Sun	R4 151	Hazyview	013 737 7311		•		•	•	Hotel; B&B

Scented Thorn Acacia (page 7)

ECO-DESTINATIONS – WITH NO BIG FIVE

NAME	*MAP REF*	*AREA*	*TEL NO*	*SIZE ha*	*SD*	*GD*	*SW*	*GW*	*W A**	*FACILITIES*
Honnet Nature Reserve	B1 ⌂ 2	Tshipise	015 539 0651			•	•		•	Bordering the greater Kuduland Safari; Youth Hostel with breakfast; rondavels and camping; electricity; self-catering; outside hot pool and 2 cold pools
Nwanedi Nature Reserve	B1 ⌂ 3	Musina	015 539 0707 015 539 0723		•		•			Beautiful mountain area, waterfalls, dams; hiking, fishing, canoeing, 4X4; small wildlife, antelope; resort facilities – camping, rondavels, restaurant
Eiland Mineral Natural Spring Spa	H2 ⌂ 13	Hans Merensky Game Reserve	015 539 0707		•	•	•	•		Nature Reserve close to Kruger; chalets and caravan/camping with electricity; self-catering; restaurant; trampoline; super tube
Thulani Safari Lodge	J4 ⌂ 19	Phalaborwa	015 781 5414	140	•	•		•		25 rooms; meals included
Ekuthuleni	L3 ⌂ 28	Hoedspruit	015 793 1657	300		•	•			14 chalets – self-catering
Giraffe Camp	M4 ⌂ 81	Acornhoek	013 792 4526	4 000		•		•		Gazebo Lodge; 12 guests; Rock Camp 10 en suite double rooms; meals included
Maduma Boma	M4 ⌂ 58	Klaserie	015 793 2813	200		•	•			7 luxurious chalets; 6-10 guests; pools
Ndabushi Bush Retreat	M4 ⌂ 49	Hoedspruit	015 793 3195	15			•			6 bungalows; self-catering
Off The Beat Safari Camp	L4 ⌂ 45	Hoedspruit	015 793 2422	60		•		•	•	Bush lodge; 8 guests; timber-thatch elevated cabins; self-catering; horse trails
Phelwana Game Lodge	M4 ⌂ 82	Acornhoek	015 793 2475	200		•		•	•	7 chalets; 6-10 guests; self-catering and bomas; self-catering facilities
Izinyoni	S6 ⌂ 165	Malelane	013 792 4555	2	•	•	•	•		Guest House; 6 guests; B&B incl
Jerusalemkop Game Farm	T4 ⌂ 156	Nelspruit	013 712 5224	1 000	•	•	•	•		Guest House, B&B incl; self-catering camping
Marloth Park	S6 ⌂ 164	Malelane	013 792 4421	1 500	•	•			•	Chalets on river; 3 rondavels; caravan and camp site; self-catering
Thanda Nani	T6 ⌂ 176	Malelane	013 792 4543	7 000		•			•	Rondavels en suite; meals included

Giraffe
(page 18)

MARCS TREE HOUSE

Chalets above ground, are the feature at Marc's Tree House – where you can see some of the Big 5

ECO-DESTINATIONS – WITH SOME BIG 5

NAME	MAP REF	AREA	TEL NO	SIZE ha	SD	GD	SW	GW	WA	FACILITIES
Makuya Park Game Reserve	A4 7	Pafuri Gate	015 966 5576 015 793 3025	17 000	•	•		•		Luxury tented camp; self-catering drives; swimming pool; kitchen; book with African Ivory Route
Nwanedi Nature Reserve	B1 3	Musina	015 539 0707	9 300	•	•		•		Accommodation and restaurant at Protea Hotel within Howard Reserve; very beautiful area – dams and waterfall; lots of game including Square-lipped Rhino; walks
Popallin Ranch	A2 1	Musina	015 534 0644	10 000		•	•	•		Chalet camps; self-catering chalets
Letaba Ranch	G4 15	Phalaborwa	015 295 2829	72	•	•		•		Safari tents; self-catering; book with African Ivory Route
Ndzalama Lodge	H2 14	Letsitele/ Tzaneen	015 307 3065	8 000	•	•				Luxury, stone and thatch, 6-chalets, en suite with air-conditioning; swimming and rock pools
Andover	N4 77	Acornhoek	015 793 2183	8 000	•					B&B; camp site; bungalows and caravan park; self-catering
Buffaloland Safaris	M4 81	Acornhoek	015 793 2823	2 000			•		•	• **Nyati Pools Tented Camp:**– cosy, rustic, Bush Camp; self-catering; fully serviced • **Giraffe Camp:**– 16-bed lodge; beautiful gardens; self catering; ideal for groups • **Motlala:**– luxury, country house setting; catered or self-catering; open lapa; 4X4 game drives; swimming pool
Hamerkop's Nest	L3 38	Hoedspruit	015 793 3198	1 200		•	•	•		Luxury tents and rondavel; self-catering
Hippo Pools	L3 37	Mica	015 793 2088	35	•		•		•	2-bed river-front houses, Hippo Cottage; guest house; self-catering
Hongonyi Private Game Lodge	M4 61	Acornhoek	015 793 2784	1 400		•	•	•		Affordable, luxury lodge en suite & family rooms; all meals incl; no Big 5 – can walk unguided
Matumi Game Lodge	M4 76	Thornybush/ Acornhoek	015 793 2452	2 000		•		•		Chalets; self-catering or meals included
Marc's Treehouse Lodge	M4 78	Klaserie	011 476 8842	10 000	•	•				Original tree houses, en suite chalets on stilts; see picture opposite
Moholoholo Mountain View	M3 47	Acornhoek	015 795 5236	500		•		•	•	11 chalets; meals included; also forest camp
Mokwalo Private Nature Reserve	M4 67	Thornybush	015 793 2168	2 000		•	•		•	Chalets; day tours organised
Phuza Moya	L3 43	Hoedspruit	015 793 1971	2 800		•		•		Overlooks Olifants River and Drakensberg escarpment; luxury, air-conditioned tents; exclusive 6-bed River Lodge with swimming pool on Olifants and Blyde river confluence; horse trails and quad bikes

SD	Self Drive
GD	Guided Drive
SW	Self Walk
GW	Guided Walk
WA	Wheelchair Access

Num Num *(Carrissa bispinosa)* are edible, but their prick is poisonous.

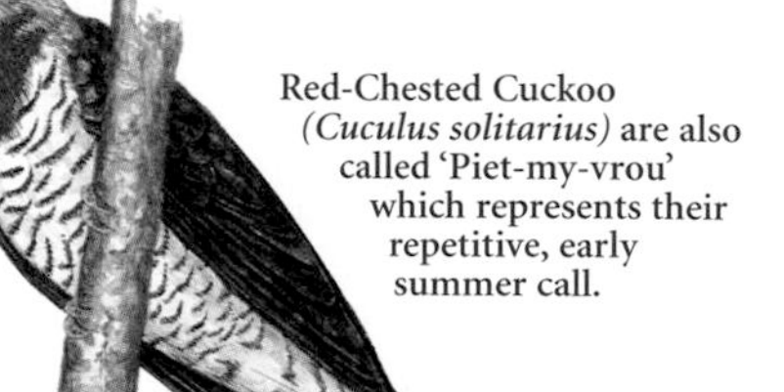

Red-Chested Cuckoo *(Cuculus solitarius)* are also called 'Piet-my-vrou' which represents their repetitive, early summer call.

BIG 5 GAME RESERVES - Grouped in Conservancies

Sandpaper Raisin *(Grewia flavescens)*

On the following pages are the premier Lowveld destinations if your interest is the Big 5. All these places also boast wonderful birds, insects, reptiles and vegetation – but with the Big 5 flavour!

BIG 5 – BALULE NATURE RESERVE

NAME	*MAP REF*	*TEL NO*	*SIZE ha*	*INTERESTING INFORMATION*
Drifters Game Lodge	L4 39	011 888 1160	30 000	Luxurious game lodge situated in pristine bush location; guests welcomed to experience the smell, sound and taste of Africa
Ezulwini	L3 31 36	011 460 0040	4 000	Olifants River traverses land – perennial flow; diverse eco-systems provide total spectrum; excellent indigenous trees; 460 species of birds identified; 4 exclusive camps – award-winning chefs
Mohlabetsi Safari Lodge	L3 40	015 793 2166	4 500	Tony and Alma welcome guests to their warm, easily accessible oasis in the bush – visitors treated as friends; game drives and bush walks reveal Big 5 and other wonders of nature; very affordable
Pondoro Lodge	L3 30	031 765 3236	4 000	New 'architecturally-designed' chalets built along Olifants River; African -style cuisine; hide overlooking dam used for 'night sleeps'; trips to Kruger and Blyde River Canyon environs can be arranged
Singwe	L3 29	015 793 3344	400	Luxury camp – River Lodge – on banks of Olifants River; unusual surround of giant fig trees; unique Birding; fishing facilities; fully inclusive service with experienced rangers
Tremisan Game Lodge	L3 35	011 476 8842	4 500	Thatched chalets en suite; rooms en suite; guest house; floodlit waterhole; traditional bushveld fare in reeded bomas with Shangaan singing and dancing; visits to neighbouring environs included

Common Duiker (page 23)

BIG 5 – EDENI (KARONGWE) PRIVATE GAME RESERVE

Ground Agama *(Agama armata)*

NAME	*MAP REF*	*TEL NO*	*SIZE ha*	*WA**	*INTERESTING INFORMATION*
Edeni Lodges	L2 22	011 883 2540 015 793 016	8 600		5-star tented camps and chalets; built on riverbank of Makhutswi River; presidential suites overlook private waterholes; 280 different species of bird identified; conference facilities
Ingwe Game Lodge	L2 24	015 383 0570 013 752 8227	9 000		Large diversity of wild life, wide spectrum of bird life; abundant fauna and flora combined with gracious living; fun of the bush experience makes for memorable stay
Kuname River Lodge	L2 21	015 383 0058	8 600		Intimate lodge situated on river; great views of river, Drakensberg escarpment; finalist in AA Awards – Game Lodge catcgory 2002/03; traditional Afrikaner table; owner-run, personal attention
Makutsi Safari Farm	L2 23 24, 25	015 383 2070	10 000	•	Only hot springs in area; natural, rustic, family-orientated camp evokes home-from-home feel; non-chemical hot pool outside, Roman bath inside; bush tennis court – termite mound surface
Wait A Little Game Ranch	L2 20	083 273 9788	8 600		Only SA Big 5 safari on horseback, use SA Boerperd breed horses, trained on elephant encounters; experienced riders only; maximum of 4; trail usually 8 days, sleeping in 3 different camps, luxury tents on platforms

* WA - Wheelchair access

BIG 5 – KAPAMA GAME RESERVE

NAME	*MAP REF*	*TEL NO*	*SIZE ha*	*WA**	*INTERESTING INFORMATION*
Kapama Lodge	M4 ⌂ 71	015 793 1038 012 804 1711	13 000	●	Equivalent to 5 star; 20 chalets; adults only; all meals incl; 2 game drives plus game walk daily; elephant-back safaris; pool; visit Hoedspruit Cheetah Breeding Station
Jabulani Camp	M4 ⌂ 54	015 793 1265 012 804 1711	13 000		Total luxury, up-market camp; very private; 2 game drives, plus a walk daily; elephant-back safaris; pool; gym, sauna and spa
Nyala House	M4 ⌂ 70	015 793 2167 012 804 1711	13 000		8-bed family house incl meals; private, personalised service; 2 guided drives and a walk daily; pool; visit Cheetah Breeding Station
Hoedspruit Safari Tented Camp	M4 ⌂ 60	015 793 1633 012 804 1711	13 000		On same premises as Centre for Endangered Species; affordable, self-catering, tented camp with ablution block, lovely braai area; tea garden

* WA - Wheelchair access

BIG 5 – MAKALALI CONSERVANCY

NAME	*MAP REF*	*TEL NO*	*SIZE ha*	*INTERESTING INFORMATION*
Garonga Camp	K2/3 ⌂ 18	082 440 3522	20 000	An experience that unwinds Safari and re-awakens the senses; sleep-out deck; take a bush bath at sunset; picnic in tree house while bird-watching over a waterhole; aroma-therapy and reflexology sala
Makalali Game Lodges	L3 ⌂ 26 27 25 L2	015 793 1720 031 566 1500	14 500	Situated along Makhutswi River; own sala on stilts; photographic excursions; bird watching safaris; star-gazing sessions, tribal dancing on request; state-of-the-art conference facilities

KRUGER NATIONAL PARK TRAILS

Coming face-to-face with a huge male lion, when on foot, is an experience of a lifetime!

Round-leaved Bloodwood (page 4)

BIG 5 – MANYELETI RESERVE

NAME	*MAP REF*	*TEL NO*	*SIZE ha*	*INTERESTING INFORMATION*
Khoka Moya	N5 ⌂ 99	011 341 0282	10 000	Safari camp set alongside river course under Tamboti trees; en suite tents in contemporary style; unfenced and wide open to African experience
Mantobeni	N5 ⌂ 101	015 793 3581 011 341 0282	23 000	Close encounters with bush without sacrificing safety or comfort; stylish, tented safari – very much in style of Hemingway's Africa; 2 game drives and 1 game walk per day
Ndzhaka Game Reserve	N5 ⌂ 103	015 295 2829 015 295 3025	23 000	Small self-catering tent camp accommodates 10; group bookings only; bring bedding and other requirements; day and night game drives and guided hikes

BIG 5 – SABI SAND WILDTUIN

Flame Lily (page 13)

NAME	*MAP REF*	*TEL NO*	*SIZE ha*	*WA**	*INTERESTING INFORMATION*
Chitwa Chitwa Game Lodges	N5 ⌂ 110	013 735 5357 013 883 1354 011 783 1858	303		Animals at your doorstep throughout day whether in lodge or out on drive; chalets overlook water; neighbourhood unfenced to Kruger
Djuma Reserve	N6 ⌂ 108	013 735 5118	9 000		Where the Big 5 roam; Galago Camp only 4-star self-catering Game camp in Sabi Sands
Elephant Plains Game Lodge	N5 ⌂ 109	013 735 5358	4 500		Children under 12 welcome at half price; all accommodation overlooks plain with waterhole where herds of game and Big 5 come to drink
Exeter Game Lodges	P5 ⌂ 121	013 735 5140	10 000		Children of all ages welcome; 5-Star lodge offering exceptional value below 5-star pricing
Idube Game Reserve	P5 ⌂ 129	013 735 5459 011 888 3713	11 000		Knowledgeable rangers; staff highly effective and helpful
Leopard Hills	P5 ⌂ 128	013 737 6626	10 000		One of smallest reserves – accommodates only 16 guests providing intimate, personalised service, home – home-from-home but still 5-star luxury; intimate, friendly camp
Lion Sands	Q6 ⌂ 144	013 735 5000 011 315 9300	3 500	•	Substantial access to perennial Sabie River; unique activities programmeastronomy, wildlife lectures, bush sleep-outs and health spa; highest standard of service; luxury facilities
Londolozi Private Game Reserve	P5 ⌂ 125 ⌂ 139	011 809 4300	15 000		One of the original Sabi Sand Reserves; trend setting member of prestigious Relais & Chateaux portfolio
Mala Mala Game Reserve	P6 ⌂ 132 ⌂ 138 ⌂ 142	013 735 5661 031 765 2900	17 000	•	Recognised as finest game-viewing destination in Africa; awarded 'Best Hotel in Africa' by Travel & Leisure magazine

Wandering Jew (page15)

NAME	*MAP REF*	*TEL NO*	*SIZE ha*	*WA**	*INTERESTING INFORMATION*
Nyati	P5 ⌂ 120	013 7351235	6 500	•	On Sand River; 10 luxury en suite chalets on sprawling lawns; fully equipped gym; professionally guided walks and drives; fine cuisine under African stars
Nkorho	N6 ⌂ 111	013 735 5367	5 500		A fresh encounter and a sense of freedom; Bush Lodge abundance of wild life
Notten's Bush Camp	P6 ⌂ 141	013 735 5105	4 000	•	Very small camp – only 8-9 guests, providing for exceptionally personalised service and unique experience
Sabi Sabi	P5 ⌂ 140 ⌂ 143	013 735 5656 011 483 3939	5 000		Reviewed as 'South Africa's Premier Game Reserve'; 3 private, uniquely different Lodges where you can experience Yesterday Today and Tomorrow – in architecture, cuisine and style
Savanna Lodge	P5 ⌂ 136	013 7355458	2500		Part of Alicecot within Sabi Sand; max 14 guests; tented lodge; game drives in open landrover; all food included; open air boma overlooking waterhole
Simbambili Game Lodge	N5 ⌂ 107	011 883 7918	4 500		Some of best leopard viewing in area; newly-built, large, luxury rooms each with plunge pool and elevated sala day-bed under thatched patio; library/meeting room, curio shop; boma
Singita Private Game Reserve	P5 ⌂ 130 ⌂ 137	011 234 0990 013 735 5456	18 000		Voted 'World's No 1 Destination' by Conde Nast Traveller readers for 2001-2002; exceptionally luxurious lodges and facilities
Ulusaba Game Lodge	P5 ⌂ 126	013 735 5608	13 500	•	Safari Lodge built on banks of dry Mabrak riverbed, in 'tree-house' style in heart of bush; Rock Lodge perched on summit of koppie with spectacular panoramic views

* WA - Wheelchair access

Lion (page 27)

Royal Malewane

At Royal Malewane, in the Thornybush Reserve, luxury runs wild.

BIG 5 – THORNYBUSH GAME RESERVE

NAME	*MAP REF*	*TEL NO*	*SIZE ha*	*WA**	*INTERESTING INFORMATION*
Chapungu Lodge	M4 53	015 793 1711	11 500		Luxurious tented suites on Monwana River; boma and dining room; rock pool, elevated viewing deck at lodge waterhole; curio shop
Kwa-Mbili Lodge	M4 62	015 793 2773	1 000		Owner-managed lodge; tasty, specialised home cooking; chalets and tents all under cool thatch; intimate, personalised, accommodating service; flexibility with any activities
Royal Malewane Game Reserve	M4 75	015 793 0150	11 500	•	An exquisite synthesis of nature's wild pulse balanced with the quiet, sophisticated sublimity of colonial comfort, elegance and style; each deck and pool looks across bushveld – ultimate privacy
Ruimte Big 5	M4 68	015 793 2751	12 000	•	Guest house; B&B; outside the Thornybush boundary, but right next door; traverse rights for game drives
Tangala Authentic Safari Camp	M4 72	015 793 0321	11 500	•	One of last remaining authentic family-run lodges, designed to be eco-friendly and electricity-free without sacrificing quality; ultimate rustic luxury; pool overlooks active waterhole
Thornybush Lodge	M4 52	015 793 1976 011 883 7918	11 500		Best value 5-star lodge in Lowveld; spa licensed by Guerlain of France; smaller lodges each with own unique character – Jackalberry, Shumbalala, n'Kaya, Serondella, Chapungu Game Lodges; marketed by Inzalo Exclusive Safari Destinations

* WA - Wheelchair access

A winter Safari with Sabi Sabi in the Sabi Sand – details on page 94

False-marula *(Lannea sweinfurthii)* have fruit that is very different to that of their look-alike, the Marula (page 3).

BIG 5 – TIMBAVATI AREA

NAME	*MAP REF*	*TEL NO*	*SIZE ha*	*WA**	*INTERESTING INFORMATION*
Akeru Private Camp	M5 92	013 7511 374 015 793 2250	8 000	•	Horseshoe of luxurious thatched bungalows overlooking waterhole; all meals incl; great value for money; minimal electricity; connected by same longitude along Nile with Egyptian Sphinx
Gomo Gomo Game Lodge	L5 88	013 752 3954	12 000	•	Part of greater Kruger built on Nhlaralumi River; both luxury tented accommodation and thatched chalets; viewing deck to river, boma dinners every evening
Inkwazi Lodge	L5 87	015 793 1836 011 730 1836	3 600	•	Very small, private camp; 2 en suite chalets, 2 en suite family chalets; tents; can selfcater but outstanding cuisine if required; outdoor boma; 2 fully qualified rangers
Kings Camp	L5 89	015 793 3633	3 000		Facilities to traverse 17 000 ha of Timbavati land; pristine and exclusive area; great attention to details of 'Whole Experience'
Motswari	L5 86	011 463 1990	20 000	•	One of original Game Reserves in Timbavati; remains in old traditional colonial style; game dinner in boma out in bush; Game Reserve open boundary with Kruger; on Sohebele River; therapy of pristine wilderness with qualified field guides
Ngala Private Game Reserve and Tented Camp	M5 93 98	011 809 4300	14 780	•	First private game concession with Kruger; 3-way partnership between non-government organisation (World-wide Life Fund), State (SANP) and private enterprise. Paved way for establishment of Transfrontier Peace Parks
Tanda Tula Safari Camp	L5 90	021 794 6500	12 000		Renowned as 'most luxurious tented camp in South Africa' by Fodor; East African tents, outdoor showers; African cuisine; private, secluded, tranquil; log fires; boma dining
Umlani Bush Camp	L5 91	012 346 4028	15 000		Wilderness experience for more adventurous travellers; bush camp built of reeds and thatch; no electricity, paraffin (kerosene) lanterns; walking a speciality

* WA - Wheelchair access

BIG 5 GAME RESERVES - not in large conservancies

NAME	*MAP REF*	*TEL NO*	*SIZE ha*	*WA**	*INTERESTING INFORMATION*
Mukuya Park – Mutale Falls Camp	A4 7	015 295 2829 015 295 3025	40 000		Safari tented camp for 10 located high on cliff above Mutale River; series of potholes downstream, water activities possible; African Ivory Route
Letaba Ranch	G4 15	015 295 2829 015 295 3025	42 000		Mtombeni Camp on banks of Great Letaba River; great views of river; walking trails; self-drives; African Ivory Route
Vienna Game Lodge	L3 44	015 793 2333	6 000		2 Lodges – all meals included; self-catering bush camp
Pezulu Tree House	M4 74	0157932724	300		Small, private conservancy; fully catered and sleep in tree houses with en suite facilities, and small balconies, built around a waterhole; plus self-catering bush camp
Tshukudu Game Lodge	L3 41	015 793 2476	5 000	•	Borders on Kruger; family orientated Lodge offers comfortable accommodation; daily walk with orphaned animals like cheetah and elephant released back into wild, but still seeking human contact; originally property of one of SA's presidents
Umhlametsi Game Reserve	L4 42	015 793 2971	6 000	•	Conservancy of 8 farms; 4 lodges provide typical pristine bushveld experience; central to everything Lowveld Tourism has to offer
Bongani Mountain Lodge	T5 162	0137641114	8000		Spectacular views in magnificent, mountainous scenery; closest Big 5 to Nelspruit; thatched cottages fully catered; highest concentration in SA of San rock art

* WA - Wheelchair access

Honeybees (page xiv)

(page xiv)

Wild Dagga *(Leonotis leonorum)* is a favourite of bees in the summer.

GOLDEN MONKEY

Elephants are a sure favourite on any game drive!

KRUGER NATIONAL PARK

Centipede
Class Diplopoda

MAIN CAMPS

Each of these camps are electrified, and have * Day Visitor Areas, shops, petrol stations and telephones.
In addition, they all have organised Day Walks and Night Drives – with trained Rangers – which can be booked in advance.

NAME	*MAP REF*	*RESTAURANT CAFETERIA*	*CAMPING CARAVAN*	*TEL NO*	*ADDITIONAL INFORMATION*
Punda Maria	B4	●	●	013 735 6873	In-camp trail; laundromat
Shingwedzi	D5	●	●	013 735 6806	** Swimming pool; Educational Display; laundromat
Letaba	H6	●	●	013 735 6636/7	Kruger Park Emergency Services; Environmental Education Centre; Educational Display; in-camp trail; laundromat
Mopani	G5	●		013 735 6536	** Swimming pool; in-camp trail; conference facilities; laundromat
Olifants	J6	●		013 735 6606/7	Educational display; laundromat
Orpen	M5			013 735 6355	Laundromat
Satara	M6	●	●	013 735 6306/7	KNP Emergency Services; Educational Display; car wash; laundromat
Berg-en-dal	S5	●	●	013 735 6106/7	** Swimming pool; in-camp trail for the blind; conference facilities; Environmental Education Centre; Educational Display; laundromat
Crocodile Bridge	S7		●	013 735 6012	Laundromat
Lower Sabie	R7	●	●	013 735 6056/7	** Swimming pool; laundromat
Pretoriuskop	R5	●	●	013 735 5128/32	** Swimming pool; in-camp trail; laundromat
Skukuza office;	Q6	●	●	013 735 5611 013 735 4000	Kruger Park Emergency Services; car hire; car wash; bank; post doctor; Environmental Education Centre; Educational Display; laundromat; swimming pools for residents and Day Visitors

* Day Visitor Areas include toilets, seating, shade and braai area
** Swimming pool for residents only

BUSH CAMPS

Each of these camps is set in beautiful surroundings and has 15 huts, fully equipped and cleaned daily. All camps have telephone facilities, and Bateleur has conference facilities. There are no shops or other services.

NAME	*MAP*	*TEL NO*
Bateleur	E4	013 735 6843
Sirheni	C4	013 735 6860
Shimuwini	H4	013 735 6683
Talamati	N6	013 735 6343
Biyamiti	S6	013 735 6171

AFRICAN IVORY ROUTE

Camaraderie around the fire on a Kruger Trail

WILDERNESS TRAILS

Kettle on the boil!

PRIVATE CAMPS (PC) or EXCLUSIVE CAMPING (EC)

(EC) These Camps have camping and caravan facilities.
(PC) To stay at these camps you must book the entire camp.

NAME	*MAP REF*	*TEL NO*	*OTHER INFORMATION*
Balule (EC)	K6	013 735 6306/7	Camp/caravan plus additional 6 huts
Boulders (PC)	G5	012 428 9111	1 house with 12 beds
Maroela (EC)	M5	013 735 6355	Only camp and caravan
Roodewaal (PC)	L6	012 428 9111	4 bungalows with 19 beds
Tamboti (EC)	M5	013 735 6355	Camp/caravan plus safari tents; toilets for disabled
Malelane (EC)	T5	013 735 6152	Camp/caravan plus additional 5 huts

Elephants
page 19

A view from a Singita chalet, across the N'wanetsi River.

KRUGER NATIONAL PARK CONCESSION LODGES

All these lodges have access to additional roadways within Kruger Park, not traversed by the general public. Most offer game drives in open vehicles that are permitted to go off road in appropriate terrain, after Big-5 sightings. Nearly all offer guided walks with trained staff.

TRAIL	*MAP REF*	*AREA*	*SIZE ha*	*TEL NO*	*WA**	*INFORMATION*
The Outpost	A4 ⌂ 8	Pafuri	2 200	0827839598		Within Kruger boundaries; also views of Zimbabwe and Mozambique; broken away from traditional lodge style – Boutique Hotel all open plan – simple, modern look in the bush; mountains all around; 4 gorges, huge canyons; great Birding
Singita Lebombo Lodge	M7 ⌂ 97	Eastern Kruger near Satara	15 000	021 683 3424 013 735 5500		15 ultra-luxury, 'elevated lofts' perched on cliffs of Nwanetsi River gorge; 12-bed fly camp; spectacular views across savannah plains through Lebombo Mountains; international wine cellar; fully equipped gym, health spa
Hamilton's Tented Camp	N6 ⌂ 115	South-east of Orpen Gate	10 000	084 505 4900 0861 000333		6 magnificent tents; superb views of Ngwenyeni Dam; raised wooden walkways amongst ancient Jackalberry trees
Imbali Safari Lodge	N6 ⌂ 116	South-east of Orpen Gate	10 000	084 505 4900 0861 000333		Luxury lodge – 12 suites on Mwatswitswonto River; game safaris, guided walks, health spa, private plunge pools with jacuzzi; bush picnics; champagne breakfasts
Rhino Post Game Lodge	P6 ⌂ 145	North of Skukuza	12 100	082 466 8538 035 474 1473	•	Specialists in guided walking safaris in Kruger; 16- and 8-bed camps as well as 'sleep-outs'; all meals included; on Mutlumuvi River
Hoyo-Hoyo Tsonga Lodge	N6 ⌂ 117	South-east of Orpen Gate	10 000	084 505 4900 0861 000333		6 thatched huts; cultural and traditional orientation to activities and events; arrivals greeted with tribal dancing
Tinga Private Game Lodge	Q6 ⌂ 146	Near Skukuza Southern KNP	4 400	0861 505050 013 735 5811		2 lodges of 9 chalets, luxury suites on Sabie River; 32 km of Sabie River; 5-star cooking with homely feel; wine cellar; riverine area with retiring nyala, bushbuck; excellent bird sightings
Jock Safari Lodge	R6 ⌂ 161	Between Skukuza and Malelane Gate	6 000	011 537 4620 013 735 5200		Luxury upmarket lodge – 24-bed, magnificent walking area amongst spectacular rocky granite outcrops – at least 12 San rock art sites here; regular superb sighting of both species of rhino
Lukimbi Safari Lodge	S6 ⌂ 166	Between Berg-en-dal & Croc Bridge	14 200	011 888 3713 011 869 9115	•	14 luxury, 2 ultra-luxury suites – 'comfortable with surroundings'; wacky, fun feeling; unusually decorated; spectacular views; good rhino country; activities tailored to individual needs
Mpanamana Lodge	S7 ⌂ 169	East of Croc Bridge	18 000	011 315 9300		Small tented camp and mud huts; very little impact on environment; near Crocodile River, close to Lebombo Mountains; grass plains; massive herds of game

* WA - Wheelchair access

TRIBAL HERITAGE SITES and CULTURAL VILLAGES

NAME	MAP REF	AREA	TEL NO	COMMENTS
Baleni Traditional Camp	F2	Giyani	015 295 3025	Visit authentic village in Mopane woodland on banks of Klein Letaba River; experience day in life of black family - food, dance, work, mining salt
Lekagape Cultural Tours	J4	Phalaborwa	083 593 9519	Cultural tour of village and refugee camp; consultation with sangoma (traditional healer); enjoy traditional meal and tribal dancing
Palabora Foundation	J4	Phalaborwa	015 7695004	Free, escorted trips into the Namakgale and Lulekane townships to see community projects in action
Nyani Tribal Village	M4	Acornhoek Area	015 793 3816	Experience the daily lives of a true Shangaan Tribe
Ebutsini Cultural Village	U4	Near Barberton	017 884 0352	Swazi village; traditional-style accommodation; tour medicinal nursery – see plants growing; receive advice on traditional remedies
Matsamo Cultural Village	U5	Jeppes Reef near Malelane	013 781 0578	Cultural experience; curio shop with crafts - weaving, pottery etc; dancing; meals; learn about Swazi culture; 4X4 drives and horseriding
Phumelani Cultural Experience	R4	Numbi Gate, Hazyview	013 798 0020	Chief Mdluli's tribe performs traditional Swazi dances including the gumboot dance; traditional buffet meal
Shangana Village	R4	Graskop Road, Hazyview	013 781 0578	Authentic African village homes; complete cultural experience of traditions
Sudwalas Kraal	T3	Nelspruit	013 733 3073	Tour village and experience Swazi, Ndebele and Zulu cultures

Curio artefacts are carved from exotic wood to protect indigenous trees.

Cultural Tourism is increasingly popular.

AFRICAN IVORY ROUTE

MUSEUMS and NATIONAL MONUMENTS

NAME	MAP REF	AREA	TEL NO	COMMENTS
Foskor Mine Museum	J4	Phalaborwa	015 789 2024	Museum highlighting history of phosphate mine and town of Phalaborwa
Barberton History Museum	U4	Barberton	013 712 4208 013 712 4281	Learn about geology, mining, inhabitants and cultural history of Barberton
Belhaven House Museum	U4	Barberton	013 712 4208 013 712 4281	Built in 1904; example of late Victorian, wealthy middle-class family's pre-fabricated home – corrugated-iron walls, pressed-iron panels; furnishings
De Kaap Stock Exchange	U4	Barberton	013 712 2121 ext: 1081/ 1061	Second stock exchange built in Barberton in 1899; façade and portico have been preserved today
Globe Tavern	U4	Barberton	013 712 4208 013 712 4281	Built in 1887; used in later years as a school, tailor's shop and store room
Lewis & Marks Building	U4	Barberton	013 712 2121 ext: 1081/ 1061	First double-storey building in Barberton; headquarters of mining magnates – Sammy Marks and Isaac Lewis
Railway bridge over Komati River	S7	Komatipoort	–	National monument; in use since construction in 1895
Komatiland Forest Museum	U4	Sabie	013 764 2423 013 7641392	Gives unique perspective of forestry industry; Mon to Fri 08h00-16h30; Sat 08h00-12h00
Samora Machel Aeroplane Crash site near Komatipoort	T7	Mbuzini Settlement	–	Monument incorporating parts of aircraft which crashed in 1986, killing Mozambican President; wind blowing through upright steel pipes creates sound like approaching aircraft
Stopforth House	U4	Barberton	013 712 4208	Original furniture and articles imported between 1886 and 1914; occupied by Stopforth family until 1983
Steam Locomotive	U4	Barberton	013 712 4208	Manufactured 1898; brought to Barberton under own steam in 1971
White River Museum	S4	White River	013 751 1540	Depicting history of area; also vintage car exhibition

HISTORICAL SITES

NAME	*MAP REF*	*AREA*	*TEL NO*	*COMMENTS*
Anglican Church	U4	Barberton	013 712 2121 *	Built 1924; original church constructed of wood/iron brought by ox-wagon from Natal
Anglo-Boer War Blockhouse	U4	Barberton	013 712 2121 *	Example of earliest British design of block-house in South Africa; built in 1901 for protection against Boer forces during Anglo-Boer War
Barberton Museum	U4	Barberton	013 712 4208	General history of Barberton, geology, mining, ethnology
Cableway, Barberton-Swaziland	U4	Barberton	013 712 2121 *	Remains of the cableway – a feat of engineering used for transporting coal from Barberton, and returning with asbestos from Swaziland
Barberton Cemetery	U4	Barberton	013 712 2121 *	Graves dating from town's early period when ethnic and religious groups were segregated
Eureka City	U4	Barberton	013 712 2121 *	4X4 guided tours of old gold mining town – 'richest gold mine' in the world; see hand-dug shafts and quarries, ruins of mine and spectacular sinkholes; tour of old racecourse
Garden of Remembrance	U4	Barberton	013 712 2121 * ext: 1081/1061	Established 1899; graves and regimental badges of fallen servicemen – SA Anglo-Boer War and WW2
'Jock of the Bushveld' Statue	U4	Barberton	013 712 2121 *	Statue of the faithful dog that travelled all over the Lowveld with Percy FitzPatrick during his days as a transport rider
Kaapsehoop Mining Village	T3	Kaapsehoop	013 734 4995	Old mining village; stay in one of the old mine houses; explore village and surrounds on foot or horseback
Magistrate's Court	U4	Barberton	013 712 2121 *	Built in 1911; housed all government departments
Masonic Temple	U4	Barberton	013 712 2121 *	Originally built as a church in 1884; taken over in 1887 by the Lodge of St John in the South
Pioneer & Agnes Mine	U4	Barberton ext: 1081/1061	013 712 2121 *	99-year-old mine; guided public tours; learn to pan gold from local prospector
Steam Locomotive	U4	Barberton	013 712 2121 *	Steam engine from 1898; example of locomotives used on the railway line to Kaapmuiden
Todd House	U4	Barberton	013 712 2121 *	1887; private residence still owned by Todd Family
Cemetery & War Memorial	U4	Barberton	013 712 2121 *	1924; memorial commemorating town's fallen sons in 2 wars: SA Anglo-Boer War and WW1

HERITAGE WALK

Barberton Information Service

* BARBERTON INFORMATION SERVICE : 013 712 2121 ext: 1081/1061

PETER THOMAS

Remains of Ox-wagon at Selati Camp, Sabi Sabi, in the Sabi Sands Wildtuin

Cape Wagtail *(Motocilla capensis)*

PETER THOMAS

The cemetary at Barberton is filled with historical interest.

The Sabie River bridge at Skukuza

HISTORICAL SITES AT KRUGER NATIONAL PARK

ERA	
BK	Beginning of Kruger
EE	European Explorers
IA	Iron Age
SA	Stone Age

The colours used on this page continue to represent the outer colours of the maps on pages 104-111. These historical sites are also marked on the maps with the icon ⚲ and these numbers listed here.
E = Era and MR = Map Reference.

	HISTORICAL SITE	E	MR
1	Bobomeni Drift	EE	A4
2	Old Pafuri tented camp site (at Picnic Site)	BK	A4
3	'Crooks Corner'	EE	A5
4	WNLA* recruiting station	EE	A5
6	Potgieter's Route	EE	B4
7	Baobab Hill	EE	B4
8	Klopperfontein Drift	EE	B4
9	Dzundwini Spring (Also Ranger J J Coetzer's quarters)	IA	C4
10	Early bore-hole (at picnic site)	BK	D5
11	Thulamela Iron Age Site	IA	A4
12	Red Rocks	EE	D5
13	Bowker Kop	EE	G5
14	Old Shawu Picnic Site (Mooi Plaas)	BK	G5
15	Das Neves' Cross	EE	H6
16	Anna Ledeboer's grave (Ranger's wife)	BK	H6
17	Engelhard plaque (Dam)	BK	J6
18	Ranger LH Ledeboer's Quarters	BK	J6
19	Masorini Historical Site	IA	J5
20	Von Wielligh's baobab	BK	J6
21	Balule (Reitz's pontoon)	IA	K6
22	Grobler plaque (Dam)	BK	L6
23	Orpen Memorial (Orpen)	BK	M5
24	Original hut at Rabelais' entrance gate (small museum)	BK	M5
25	William Lloyd's grave	BK	M6
26	Trichardt's memorial	EE	N7
27	Ranger Harry Wolhuter's lion attack plaque	BK	N7
28	Sausage tree where ranger GCS Crous erected his 'wattle-and-daub' quarters (at Tshokwane)	BK	P7
29	Kruger Memorial Tablets	BK	P6
30	Orpen Memorial Koppie	BK	P6
31	Acknowledgement to Rangers (Paul Kruger Gate)	BK	Q5
32	Paul Kruger monument (Paul Kruger Gate)	BK	Q5
33	Albasini Ruins/information display	EE	R4
37	Stevenson-Hamilton memorial library and information centre	BK	Q6
38	Board Member WA Campbell hut/museum	BK	P6
40	Struben Cottage (Skukuza)	BK	Q6
41	Papenfus' clock tower (Skukuza)	BK	Q6
42	Memorial to honour the founders of KNP	BK	Q6
43	Pontoon crossing	BK	Q6
44	Selati line and rail bridge	BK	Q6
45	Selati train restaurant and museum (Skukuza)	BK	Q6
48	Prospectors' graves	EE	Q6
49	Jock of the Bushveld plaque	EE	R4
50	Pretorius' grave	EE	R4
52	'Wattle-and-daub' hut built for tourists 1930 (Pretoriuskop)	BK	R5
53	Wolhuter's windmill	BK	R5
54	Board Member Joe Ludorf plaque (Napi Kop)	BK	R5
55	Stevenson-Hamilton memorial & 'grave' (Shirimantanga Koppie)	BK	R6
56	Bushman paintings (Wolhuter Trail)	SA	R6
57	Old Delagoa - Lydenburg wagon road	EE	R6
58	Albasini's trading post (Lower Sabie)	EE	R7
59	Duke's Windmill	BK	R7
60	Sardelli's store	EE	S7
61	Francois de Cuiper's attack	EE	S7
62	Crocodile River railway bridge	BK	S7
63	Bushman paintings (Crocodile Bridge Hippo Pool)	SA	S7
64	Old Trade Route	EE	S6
65	Alf Robert's trading store	EE	S6
66	General Ben Viljoen's attack site	BK	S6
67	Outspan plaques	EE	S6
68	Jock of the Bushveld & Sable Statue (Jock Safari Lodge)	EE	R6
69	Outspan plaque	EE	S5
70	First concrete dam (Ntomeni Spruit)	BK	S5
71	Jock of the Bushveld's birthplace	EE	R5
73	Thomas Hart's grave	EE	S5
74	Stol's Nek (on Wolhuter Trail)	EE	S5

WNLA* was the mine labour recruiting body

Tsonga woman dressed in traditional attire.

ARTS, CRAFTS and CURIOS

NAME	MAP REF	LOCATION	TEL NO	COMMENTS
Feldman's Silks	P3	Pilgrim's Rest	013 767 1665	Work of local women – hand-stitched Mopane Worm silk teddy bears from silk spun in factory in Graskop
Monsoon Gallery	M3	Hoedspruit	015 795 5425	Showcase for African rural art and culture; ethnic jewellery; African décor; folk embroidery
The Green Door	M3	Hoedspruit	015 793 0216	African curios; safari clothes & shoes; post point
Tsinini Silk Farm & Weavery	P3	Graskop	013 767 1665	Silk goods made on site
Van der Waal Furniture	P3	Graskop	013 238 0029	Furniture with an 'Out of the Bush' character; manufactured by 6th-generation Ohrigstad residents
Arkas Textiles	R4	Hazyview	013 750 1996	Textile factory, furniture factory and renovators; purchase items from the on-site shop
Arkas Textiles	S4	White River	013 751 3551	African art and textiles; custom-made furniture
Artists Café & Guest House	S3	Hendriksdal on the R37	013 764 2309	Central to all activities; secluded in pine plantation; buy local and tribal art; between Nelspruit and Sabie
Bone Idle	S4	White River	013 751 2904	Bone and horn furniture and jewellery manufacturers
Bosch Ceramic Studio	S4	White River	013 751 2859	Architectural and individual works; commissions undertaken; showroom open to the public
Casterbridge Farm Centre	S4	White River	013 751 1540	Tourist retail development; individual outlets styled to showcase exceptional wares; many products manufactured locally and on Casterbridge Farm; works of local artists available
Copper Craft	T3	Rockys Drift outside Nelspruit	013 758 1194	Copper and silver jewellery; cutlery with an ethnic flavour
Elmswood outside Nelspruit	S3	Lydenburg Road	013 755 1323	Country furniture; area of exquisite vistas; safe play-ground with petting zoo for children
Eloff Gallery	S4	Casterbridge Farm Centre, White River	013 750 1282	Artworks; ceramics; furniture by local artists
Eric Stalls	T3	Nelspruit	013 733 4043	Curios; local artworks
Halls Gateway	T3	Nelspruit	013 755 6040	Buy local fare and artworks while you fill up with fuel and refreshments
Kaapsehoop	T3	Kaapsehoop	013 734 4161	Historical village; local arts and crafts
Kingdom of Africa Centre	S4	White River	013 750 1204	Crafts; curios; locally manufactured quality furniture
Kraal Kraft & Village	S4 – T3	Between White River and Nelspruit	013 758 1229	African curios; local art
QT Designer Leather	S4	White River	013 751 3270	Hats, bags, clothing made from South African leather; locally made copper jewellery
Rottcher Wineries	S4 – T3	Between White River and Nelspruit	013 751 3884	Nut factory and winery; pony rides to keep children busy
Shagana Cultural Village	R4	Hazyview	013 737 7000	Shangaan village; Sangoma; cultural show; Marula craft market
Sleeperwood	S4	White River	013 750 0763	Furniture made from various railway-sleeper woods; curios; wooden artefacts
Tsakani Silk Weavers	S4	White River	013 755 3213	High-quality locally produced silk products; Mon to Fri 9h00–15h00; weekends by appointment only
Willowbrook Cotton	S4	White River	013 751 3368	Locally manufactured and embroidered linen

Exquisite wildlife sculptures are found in many galleries the Lowveld. This sable is by Bruce Little phone (011) 880 3404

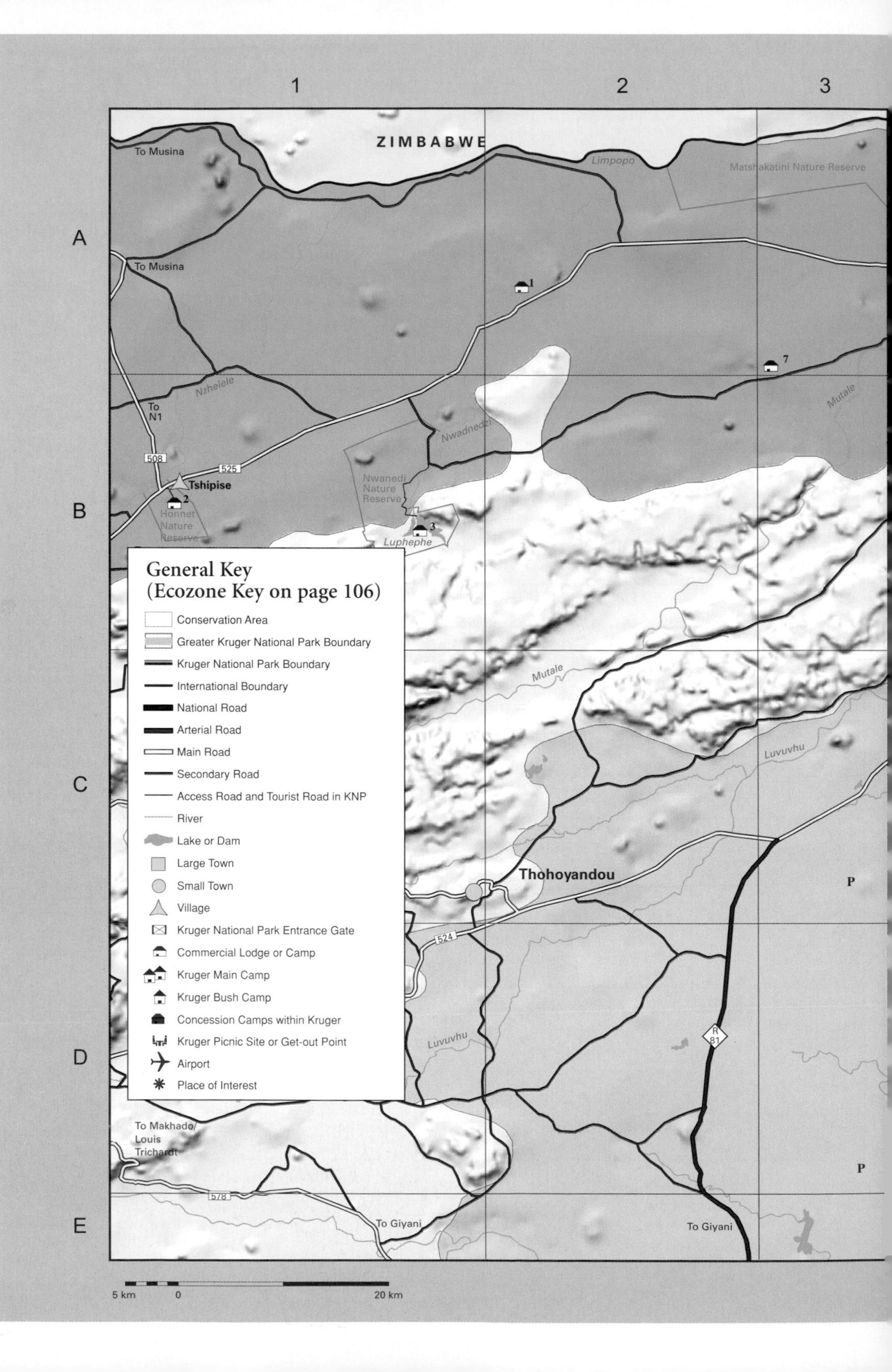

1
2
3
A
B
C
D
E
ZIMBABWE
To Musina
Limpopo
Matshakatini Nature Reserve
To Musina
1
7
Nzhelele
To
N1
Nwadnedzi
Mutale
508
525
Tshipise
2
Honnet
Nature
Reserve
Nwanedi
Nature
Reserve
3
Luphephe
General Key
(Ecozone Key on page 106)
Conservation Area
Greater Kruger National Park Boundary
Kruger National Park Boundary
International Boundary
National Road
Arterial Road
Main Road
Secondary Road
Access Road and Tourist Road in KNP
River
Lake or Dam
Large Town
Small Town
Village
Kruger National Park Entrance Gate
Commercial Lodge or Camp
Kruger Main Camp
Kruger Bush Camp
Concession Camps within Kruger
Kruger Picnic Site or Get-out Point
Airport
Place of Interest
Mutale
Luvuvhu
Thohoyandou
P
524
R
81
Luvuvhu
To Makhado/
Louis
Trichardt
P
578
To Giyani
To Giyani
5 km
0
20 km

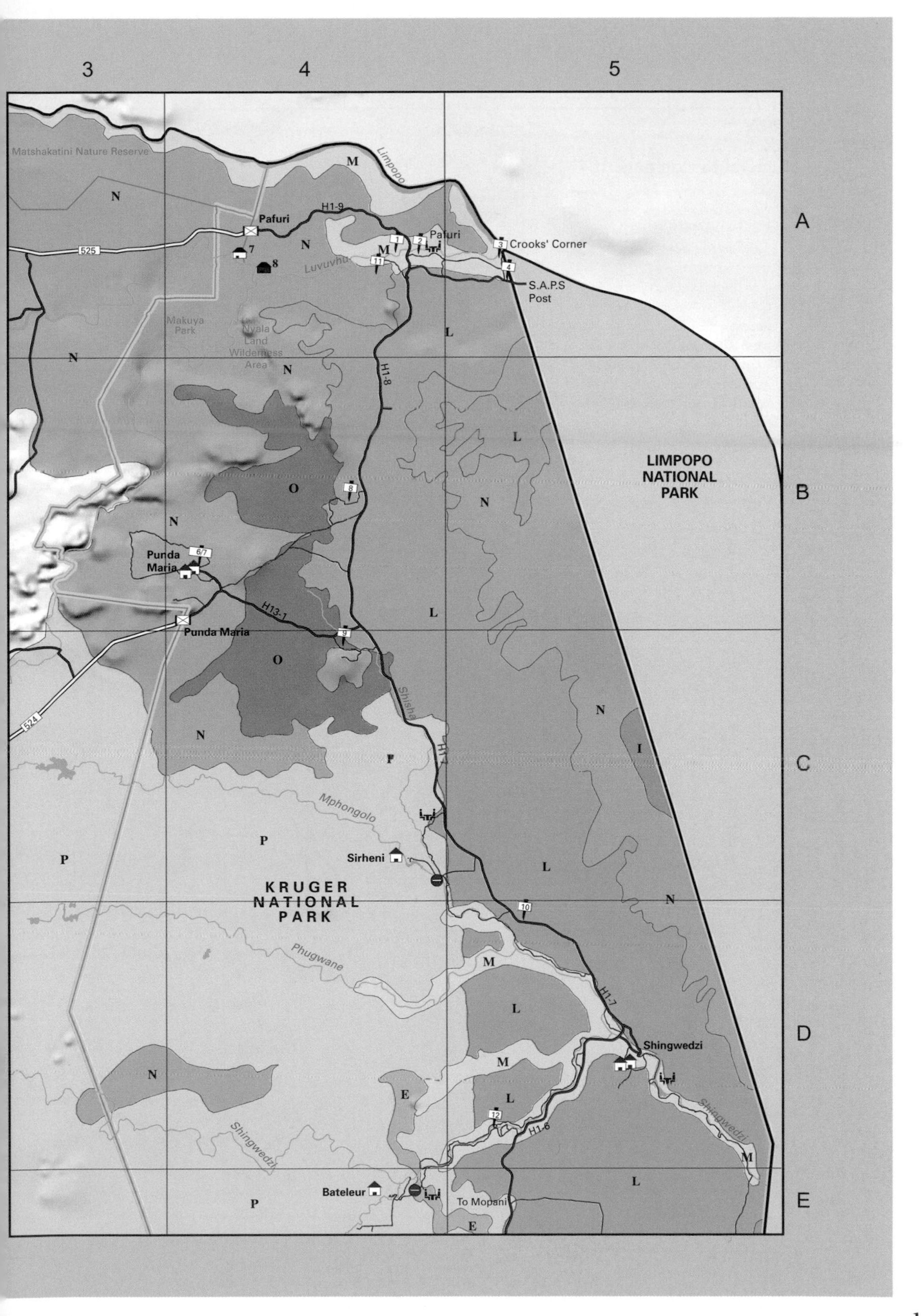
3
4
5
A
B
C
D
E
Matshakatini Nature Reserve
Limpopo
Pafuri
H1-9
525
Luvuvhu
Crooks' Corner
S.A.P.S
Post
Makuya
Park
Nyala
Land
Wilderness
Area
H1-8
LIMPOPO
NATIONAL
PARK
Punda
Maria
6/7
H13-1
Punda Maria
524
Shisha
H1-7
Mphongolo
Sirheni
KRUGER
NATIONAL
PARK
Phugwane
Shingwedzi
H1-6
Shingwedzi
Bateleur
To Mopani

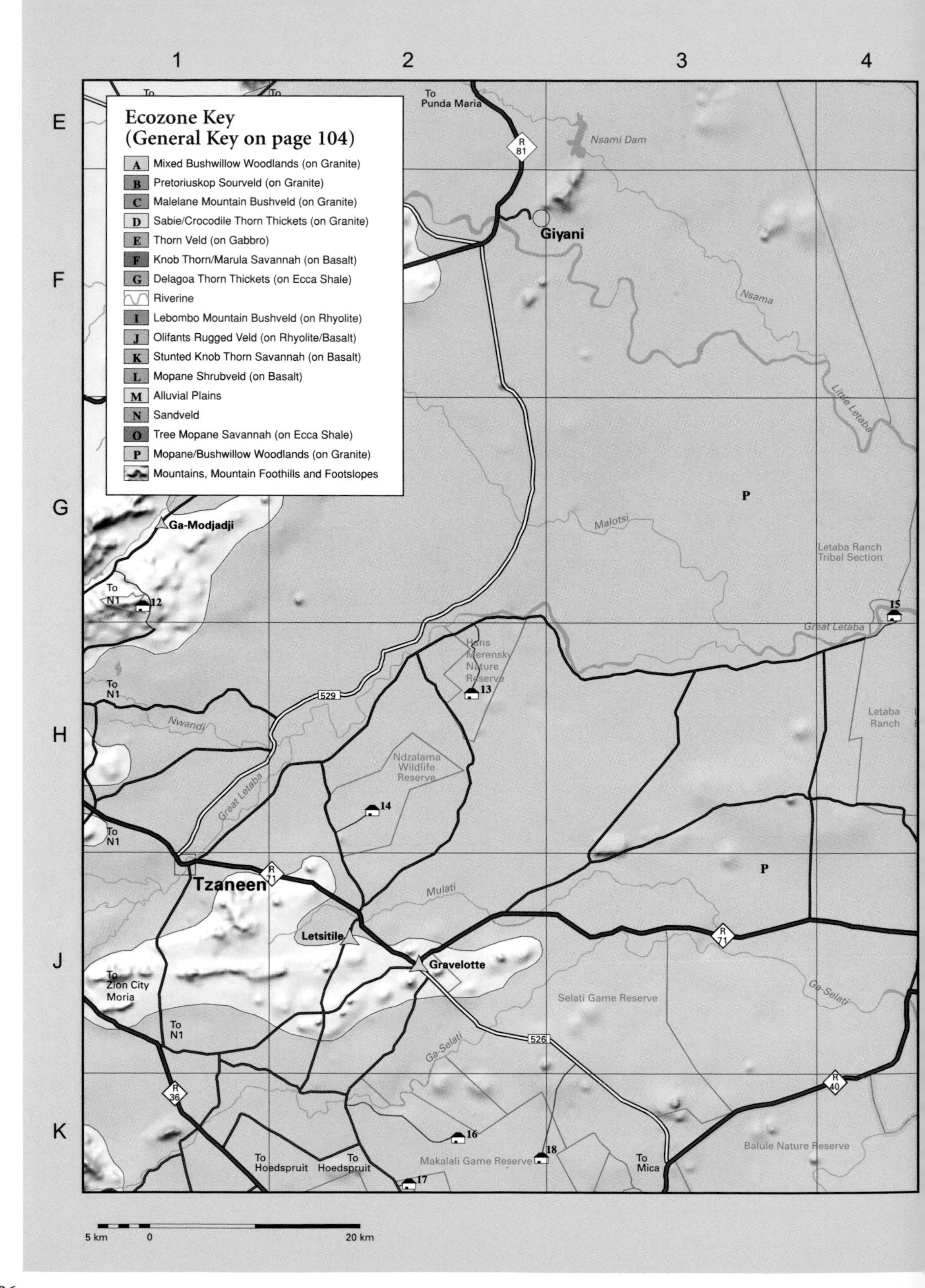

Ecozone Key
(General Key on page 104)
A Mixed Bushwillow Woodlands (on Granite)
B Pretoriuskop Sourveld (on Granite)
C Malelane Mountain Bushveld (on Granite)
D Sabie/Crocodile Thorn Thickets (on Granite)
E Thorn Veld (on Gabbro)
F Knob Thorn/Marula Savannah (on Basalt)
G Delagoa Thorn Thickets (on Ecca Shale)
Riverine
I Lebombo Mountain Bushveld (on Rhyolite)
J Olifants Rugged Veld (on Rhyolite/Basalt)
K Stunted Knob Thorn Savannah (on Basalt)
L Mopane Shrubveld (on Basalt)
M Alluvial Plains
N Sandveld
O Tree Mopane Savannah (on Ecca Shale)
P Mopane/Bushwillow Woodlands (on Granite)
Mountains, Mountain Foothills and Footslopes
1
2
3
4
E
F
G
H
J
K
To Punda Maria
R 81
Nsami Dam
Giyani
Nsama
Little Letaba
P
Malotsi
Letaba Ranch Tribal Section
15
Great Letaba
Ga-Modjadji
To N1
12
Hans Merensky Nature Reserve
13
529
Nwandi
Letaba Ranch
Ndzalama Wildlife Reserve
14
Great Letaba
To N1
R 71
Tzaneen
P
Mulati
Letsitile
Gravelotte
R 71
To Zion City Moria
To N1
Selati Game Reserve
Ga-Selati
Ga-Selati
526
R 40
R 36
16
18
To Hoedspruit
To Hoedspruit
Makalali Game Reserve
17
To Mica
Balule Nature Reserve
5 km
0
20 km

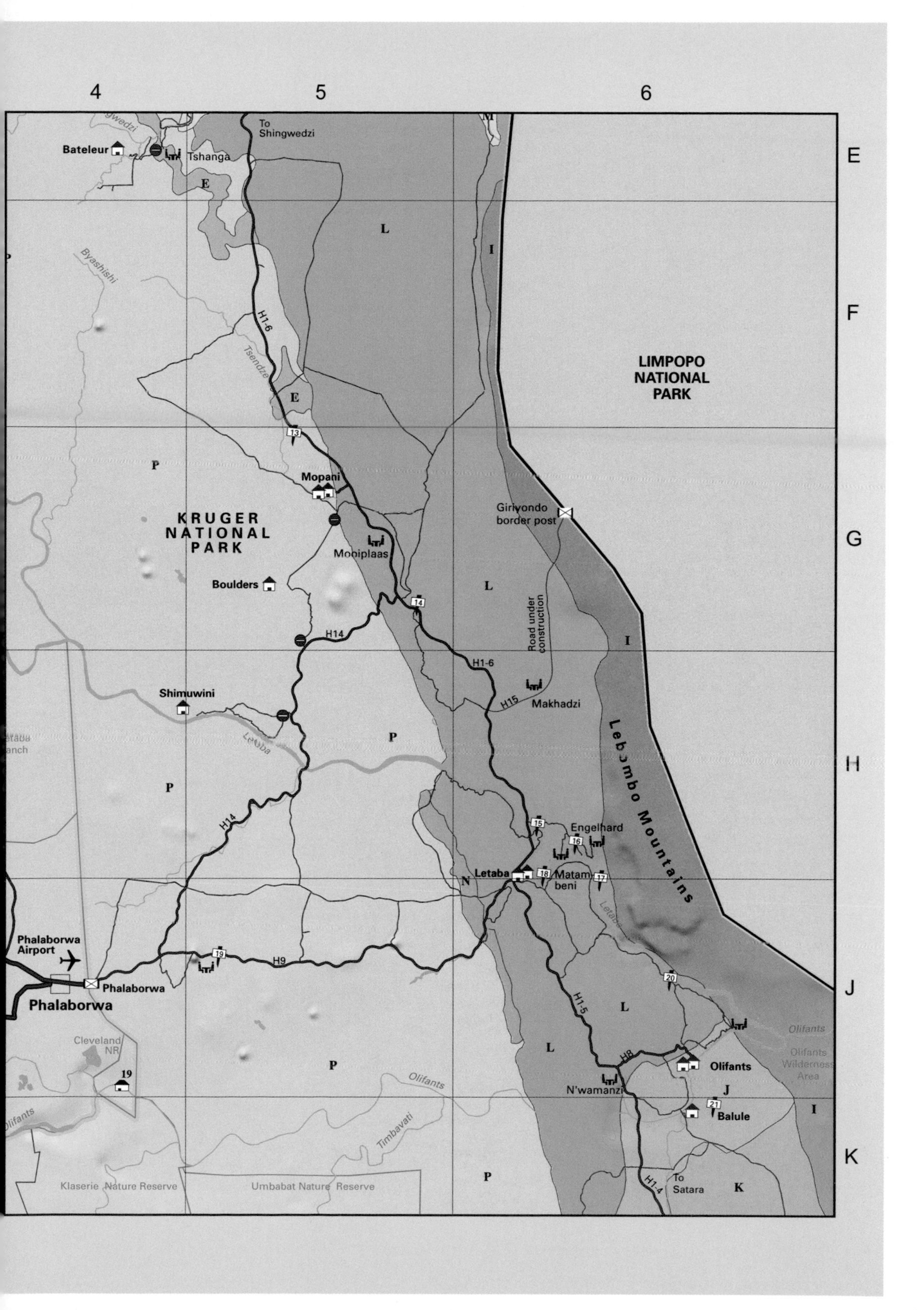

4
5
6
E
F
G
H
J
K
To Shingwedzi
Bateleur
Tshanga
Byashishi
Tsendze
H1-6
LIMPOPO NATIONAL PARK
KRUGER NATIONAL PARK
Mopani
Mooiplaas
Boulders
Giriyondo border post
Road under construction
H14
Shimuwini
Letaba
H15
Makhadzi
Lebombo Mountains
Engelhard
Letaba
Matambeni
Phalaborwa Airport
Phalaborwa
H9
H1-5
H8
Olifants
N'wamanzi
Balule
Olifants Wilderness Area
Cleveland NR
Olifants
Timbavati
Klaserie Nature Reserve
Umbabat Nature Reserve
To Satara
H1-4

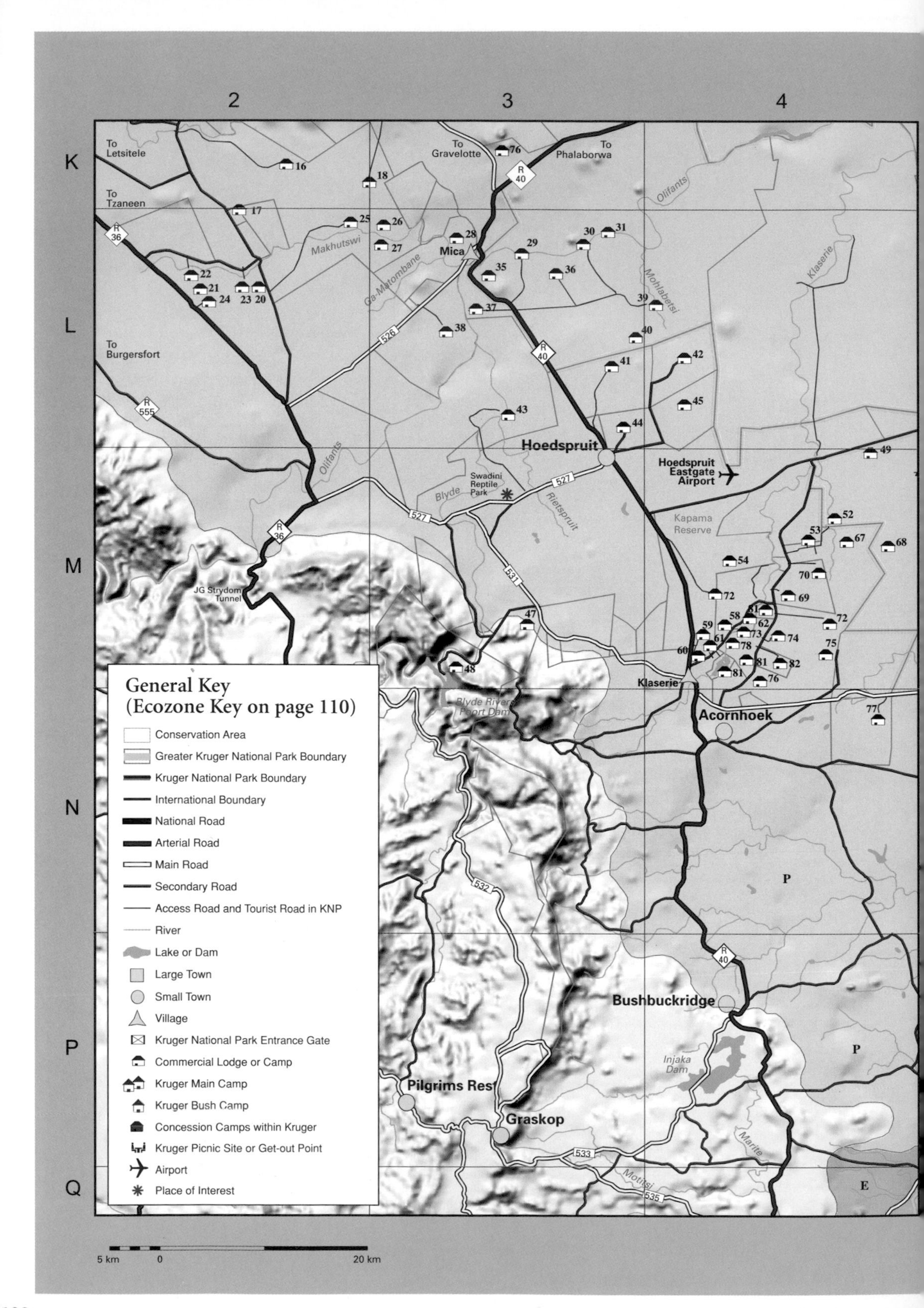

2
3
4
K
L
M
N
P
Q
To Letsitele
To Tzaneen
To Burgersfort
To Gravelotte
To Phalaborwa
Mica
Hoedspruit
Hoedspruit Eastgate Airport
Kapama Reserve
Swadini Reptile Park
JG Strydom Tunnel
Blyde River Poort Dam
Klaserie
Acornhoek
Bushbuckridge
Injaka Dam
Pilgrims Rest
Graskop
Makhutswi
Ga-Motombane
Olifants
Mohlabetsi
Klaserie
Blyde
Rietspruit
Marite
Motitsi
General Key
(Ecozone Key on page 110)
Conservation Area
Greater Kruger National Park Boundary
Kruger National Park Boundary
International Boundary
National Road
Arterial Road
Main Road
Secondary Road
Access Road and Tourist Road in KNP
River
Lake or Dam
Large Town
Small Town
Village
Kruger National Park Entrance Gate
Commercial Lodge or Camp
Kruger Main Camp
Kruger Bush Camp
Concession Camps within Kruger
Kruger Picnic Site or Get-out Point
Airport
Place of Interest
5 km
0
20 km

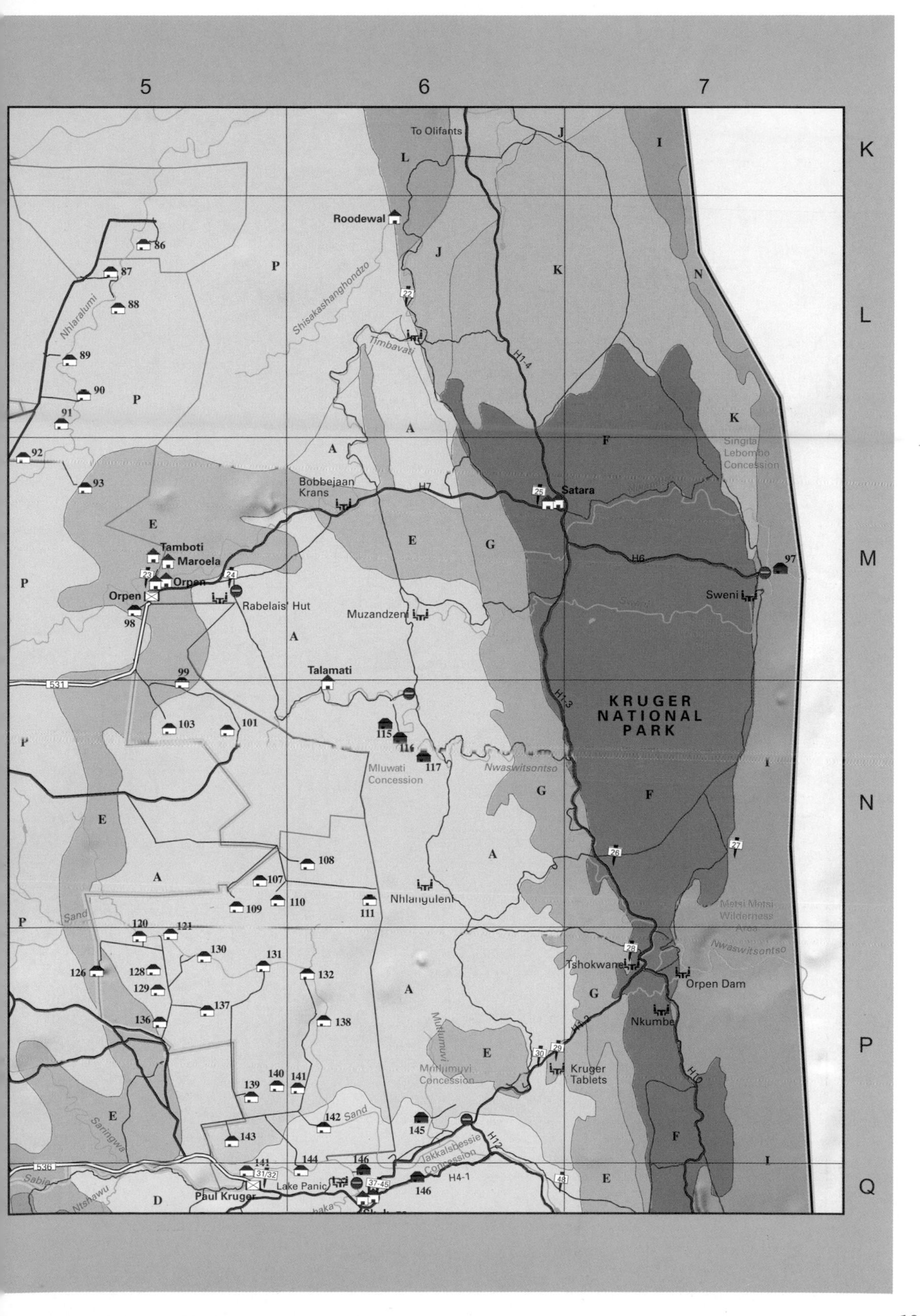

5
6
7
K
L
M
N
P
Q
To Olifants
Roodewal
Shisakashanghondzo
Nhlaralumi
Timbavati
H1-4
Singita Lebombo Concession
Bobbejaan Krans
H7
Satara
Tamboti
Maroela
Orpen
Rabelais' Hut
Muzandzeni
H6
Sweni
Talamati
531
KRUGER NATIONAL PARK
H1-3
Mluwati Concession
Nwaswitsontso
Nhlanguleni
Metsi Metsi Wilderness Area
Tshokwane
Orpen Dam
Nkumbe
Mutlumuvi
Mutlumuvi Concession
Kruger Tablets
H1-2
H10
Sand
Saringwa
Jakkalsbessie Concession
H12
H4-1
Lake Panic
Paul Kruger
Sabie
Ntshawu
536

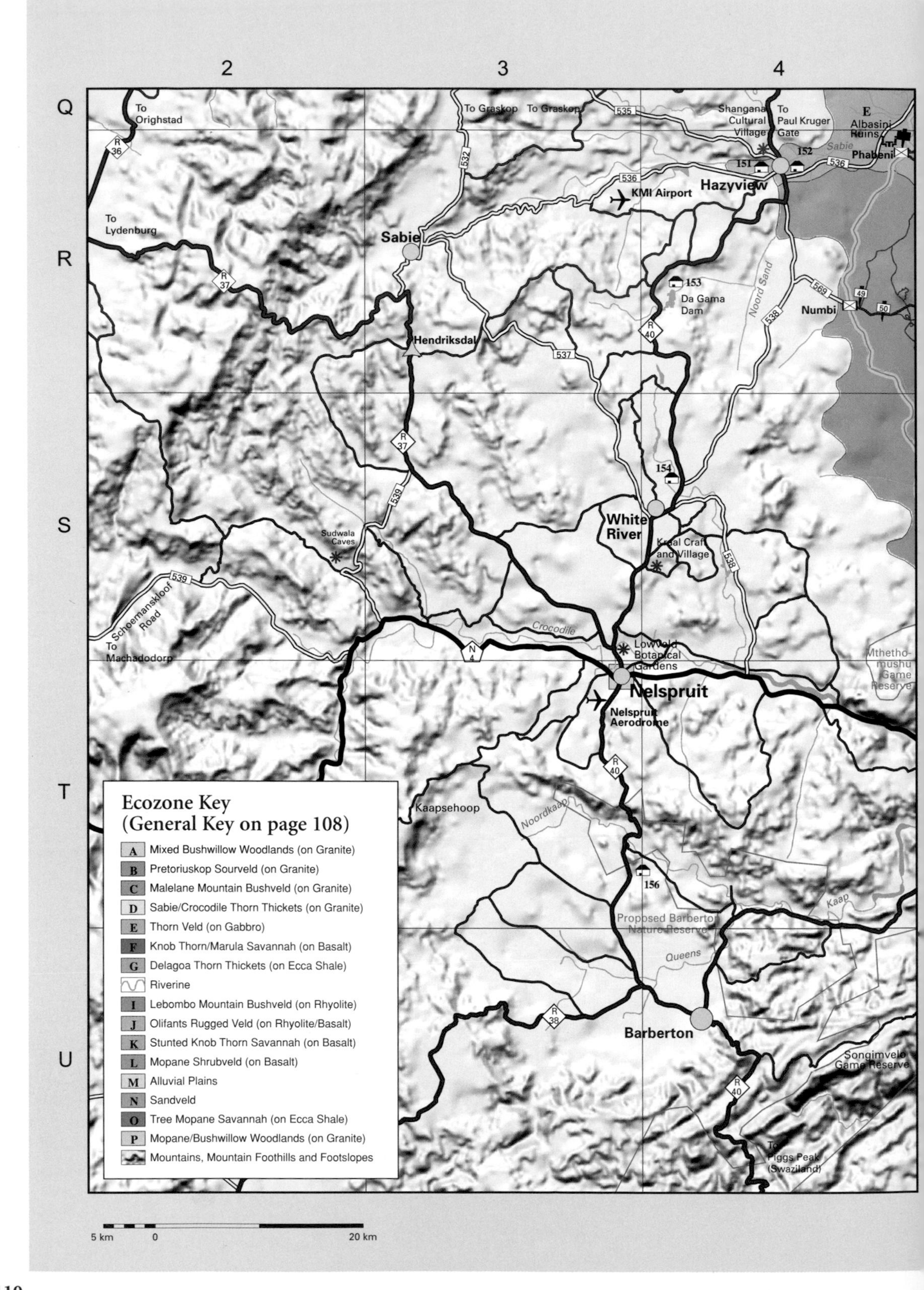
2
3
4
Q
R
S
T
U
To Orighstad
To Graskop
To Graskop
Shangana Cultural Village
To Paul Kruger Gate
E
Albasini Ruins
Phabeni
Sabie
Hazyview
KMI Airport
To Lydenburg
Sabie
Da Gama Dam
Noord Sand
Numbi
Hendriksdal
White River
Kraal Craft and Village
Sudwala Caves
Schoemanskloof Road
To Machadodorp
Crocodile
Lowveld Botanical Gardens
Nelspruit
Nelspruit Aerodrome
Mthethomushu Game Reserve
Kaapsehoop
Noordkaap
Proposed Barberton Nature Reserve
Kaap
Queens
Barberton
Songimvelo Game Reserve
To Piggs Peak (Swaziland)
Ecozone Key
(General Key on page 108)
A Mixed Bushwillow Woodlands (on Granite)
B Pretoriuskop Sourveld (on Granite)
C Malelane Mountain Bushveld (on Granite)
D Sabie/Crocodile Thorn Thickets (on Granite)
E Thorn Veld (on Gabbro)
F Knob Thorn/Marula Savannah (on Basalt)
G Delagoa Thorn Thickets (on Ecca Shale)
Riverine
I Lebombo Mountain Bushveld (on Rhyolite)
J Olifants Rugged Veld (on Rhyolite/Basalt)
K Stunted Knob Thorn Savannah (on Basalt)
L Mopane Shrubveld (on Basalt)
M Alluvial Plains
N Sandveld
O Tree Mopane Savannah (on Ecca Shale)
P Mopane/Bushwillow Woodlands (on Granite)
Mountains, Mountain Foothills and Footslopes
5 km
0
20 km

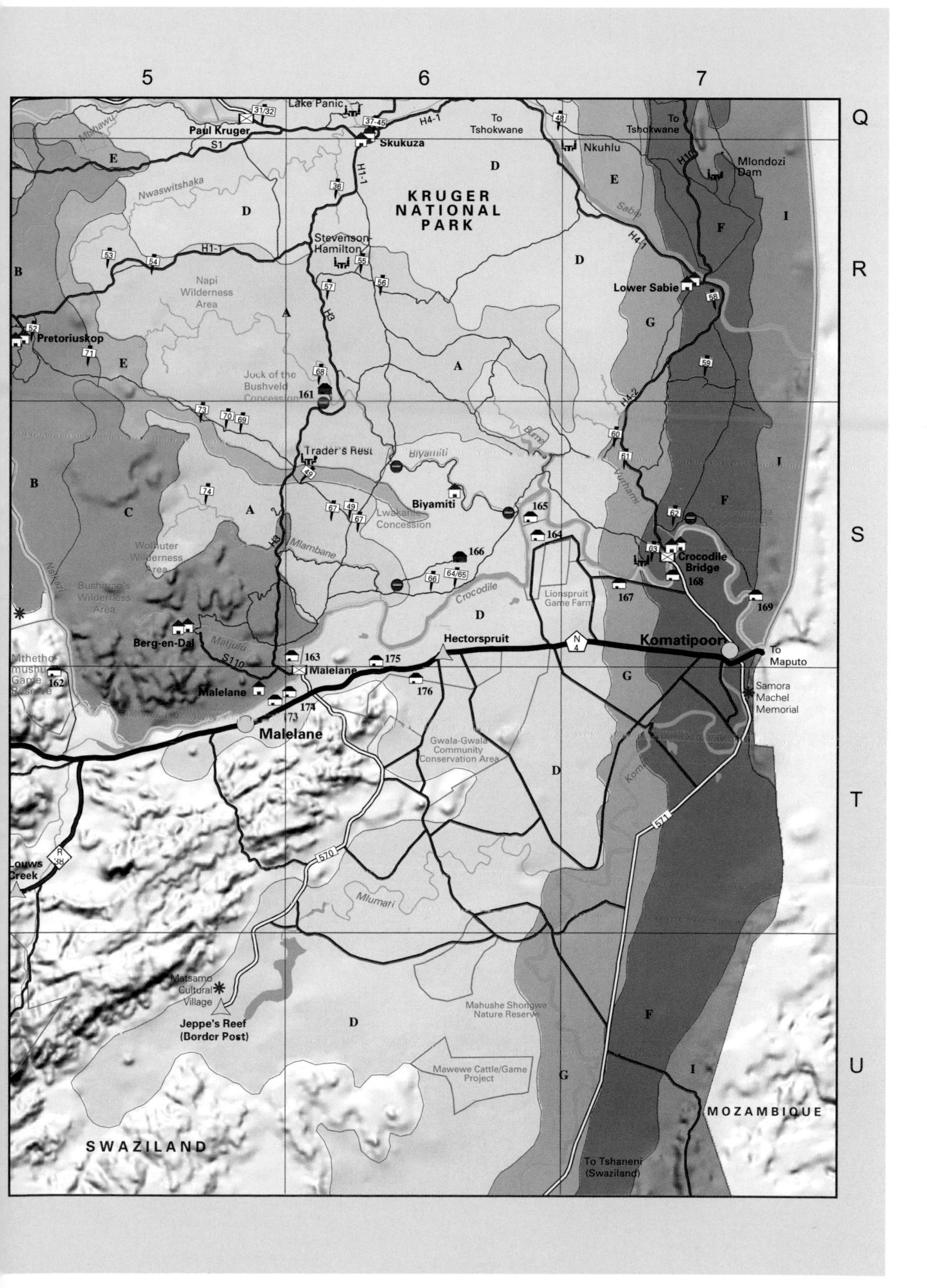
5
6
7
Q
R
S
T
U
KRUGER NATIONAL PARK
Lake Panic
Paul Kruger
Skukuza
To Tshokwane
To Tshokwane
Nkuhlu
Mlondozi Dam
Stevenson-Hamilton
Napi Wilderness Area
Lower Sabie
Pretoriuskop
Jock of the Bushveld Concession
Trader's Rest
Biyamiti
Lwakahle Concession
Wolhuter Wilderness Area
Bushman's Wilderness Area
Berg-en-Dal
Crocodile Bridge
Lionspruit Game Farm
Hectorspruit
Komatipoort
To Maputo
Samora Machel Memorial
Malelane
Mthethomusha Game Reserve
Gwala-Gwala Community Conservation Area
Louws Creek
Mlumari
Matsamo Cultural Village
Jeppe's Reef (Border Post)
Mahushe Shongwe Nature Reserve
Mawewe Cattle/Game Project
MOZAMBIQUE
SWAZILAND
To Tshaneni (Swaziland)
Nwaswitshaka
Biyamiti
Mlambane
Crocodile
Matjulu
Sabie
Vurhami
Nsikazi
Mtshawu
S1
H1-1
H4-1
H1-2
H3
H4-2
S110
N4
R38
570
571
H10
A
B
C
D
E
F
G
I
161
162
163
164
165
166
167
168
169
173
174
175
176

Fever Tree Acacia
(Acacia xanthophloea)

INDEX

Fever Tree Acacia
(Acacia xanthophloea)

Yellow-throated Longclaw *(Macronyx croceus)*

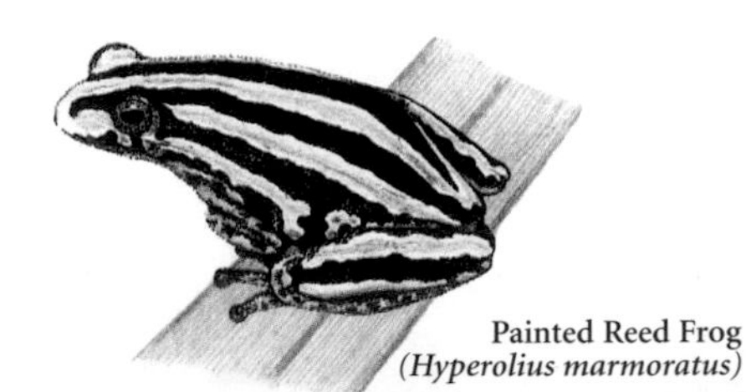
Painted Reed Frog *(Hyperolius marmoratus)*

Mistletoe
(Viscum rotundifolium)

Plains Zebra
(page 21)

NOTES

NOTES

Notes

Notes